KU-486-882

ALL THE SCULPTURE OF
MICHELANGELO

VOLUME ELEVEN
in the
Complete Library of World Art

The Complete Library of World Art

ALL THE SCULPTURE

OF MICHELANGELO

By FRANCO RUSSOLI

Translated from the Italian by
PAUL COLACICCHI

OLDBOURNE
London

Printed in Great Britain by
Jarrold and Sons Ltd, Norwich

CONTENTS

MICHELANGELO BUONARROTI

Life and Work

VASARI tells us that toward the end of the fifteenth century Lorenzo de' Medici (the Magnificent) had decorated his garden in the Piazza di San Marco with "many beautiful old pieces" and with "good ancient statues of marble and paintings and other such things, made by the best masters ever found in Italy or abroad." Lorenzo put the sculptor Bertoldo in charge of these treasures, not so much as a custodian but because "he ardently wished to found a school of painters and very good sculptors, and he wanted Bertoldo to be their master and guide, for Bertoldo had been a pupil of Donatello."

In the early part of 1489, this school, which had developed under the auspices of an enlightened and scholarly humanism, received a new pupil, brought there by Francesco Granacci: the fourteen-year-old Michelangelo di Lodovico Buonarroti (born at Caprese on March 6, 1475). He was an unusual boy who had won the admiration and, some hinted, the envy of Domenico Ghirlandaio, to whose workshop he was bound by a three-year contract drawn up on April 1, 1488. The boy was outstanding, not only for his extraordinary technical capacity, proved by copies, drawings from nature, and even breathtaking counterfeits, but also for his disquieting tendency to work independently, choosing his own examples and models, finding his own means of expression, the standards for which were no clearer to his masters than to

7

his fellow-students. One day, according to Vasari, Ghirlandaio caught sight of some drawings by Michelangelo and was "astonished by the new manner and capacity for imitation, and that a boy of such tender years could have received such a gift from God." His astonishment is understandable when we remember Ghirlandaio's own softer, naturalistic style, for we may well imagine how those drawings were aimed even then at capturing the firm structure, the absolute plastic essence of each object and figure.

That is not to claim that in these early attempts Michelangelo had already sounded the tragic depths of his later work, when he discovered a style and an image to embody the vital force he felt in reality: that image is, of course, man himself. Reports that he copied Schongauer's prints, that he drew naturalistic scenes and studies of the frescoes of the fourteenth and fifteenth centuries only confirm that Michelangelo, like all apprentices, tried his hand at many styles.

Ghirlandaio's keen and experienced eye could well have seen, as Vasari says, in the youth's few exercises, his prodigious capacity for solving any representational problem and, more important perhaps, the signs of the "new manner," or "new rendering," which were already becoming evident. The young artist was breaking free from the old canons and rules by violating them. Ghirlandaio could not, therefore, have been surprised when Michelangelo did not return to his workshop after he had been introduced to the ambience of the Medici Gardens. He must have understood that among those "old things" the boy had finally found examples of compelling form that he could emulate enthusiastically.

But in the principles of Donatello, so severely taught the young artists by Bertoldo, only an intelligence as fine as

Michelangelo's could recognize the implications of freedom. The ancient statuary was not merely a model for dry exercises, but rather a source of fresh inspiration. His first sculptures (now lost)—some terracotta figures executed in competition with Torrigiani, and the head of a *Faun*, copied from an ancient model which Lorenzo the Magnificent greatly admired—were proofs of the boy's remarkable technique which, under Bertoldo's guidance, was now directed towards imitating the ancient masters rather than copying German prints. But other works, completed shortly after, have come down to us, and we can see from them that Michelangelo's attitude toward classical art had reached a critical turning-point. He was not merely imitating, but rather interpreting; he was seeking a live, not rhetorical, form and we can observe the hints of the stylistic and moral themes that were later to mold his style.

These are the two bas-reliefs in the Casa Buonarroti at Florence: the *Madonna della Scala* and *The Battle of Centaurs*, both finished before Lorenzo's death in April 1492, while Michelangelo was his guest. Lorenzo treated him like an adopted son, and brought him into the circle of great humanists who used to meet at the Palace in the Via Larga: Poliziano, Ficino, Beniveni, Landino and Pico. While he lived in the Medici Palace, Michelangelo would often visit Santa Croce and the Carmine churches, where he would sketch in a notebook his impressions of the masterpieces of Giotto and Masaccio, both of whom, of course, had been responsible for elevating the human figure to artistic importance.

In these two reliefs we can already observe a persuasive blending of the cultural elements that influenced Michelangelo's style. Christian themes and pagan myths, the worship of the old alongside the new humanism, traces of

Giotto and the two Pisanos, Masaccio's fierceness, Donatello's burning energy, all combine to form the "new image." Detached from any particular time or place, grandiose human figures express by the tension of their formidable bodies and by their tormented effort to struggle free from the weight of stone, Man's proud but desperate consciousness that he bears within himself the motive force of an always changing universe.

Bertoldo must have been just as astonished as Domenico Ghirlandaio if, before his death, he saw the flattened relief in marble, the *Madonna della Scala*, where the young sculptor showed no consciousness of having applied Donatello's principle of shallow relief and appeared to have followed his teachings only in a few technical points. Nor could Bertoldo have perceived the closer link now existing between his master and his pupil, in other words the capacity for expressing not only a natural space vibrant with light, or the vital arabesque of a moving body, but above all rendering Man in his stoic dignity. The technique of flattening was not used here by Michelangelo for representation or rhythm merely, but to stress, by compressing one plane upon the other, the clash between his forms. Enclosed between the monumental steps and the block upon which she is seated, the Virgin—described by Tolnay as "the archetype of Woman, creator of life and guardian of death"—holds her struggling Child to her breast; He tries to escape from her hands (which have been dramatically foreshortened). The Child's herculean back already suggests the rhetorical use of dimension that we find, fully developed, in the figure of *Day* (the Medici Tombs).

A desperate energy, controlled within the extended planes of the *Madonna della Scala*, was to be unleashed in the more contorted *Battle of Centaurs*. The legend was probably suggested to Michelangelo by Poliziano, who appeared to understand which themes from mythology could best serve the youth's creative urge. Michelangelo refused to perform the elaborate, sterile exercise of copying the ancient sarcophagi in his teacher Bertoldo's manner. Nor would he imitate the exaggerated and harsh anatomies that everywhere appear in the works of Pollaiolo and Verrocchio. *The Battle of Centaurs* is a fairly high-relief with much of the energy of ancient Greek marbles, and one can detect a lesson or two from Nicola Pisano. The fighters' bodies emerge fully formed from the rough background, offering ample surfaces and projections for dramatic value.

Shortly after this work was completed, Lorenzo de' Medici died. Michelangelo returned to his father's home, where he carved a large statue of *Hercules*. This was unfortunately lost, with other works of the same period, among which biographers record a wooden *Crucifix* for the Prior of Santo Spirito, who furnished him "dead bodies to improve his knowledge of anatomy, which was the only favor he could do in return for the artist's work." Meanwhile, Piero de' Medici had called him to his court and accorded him the same honors his father had, though his lack of imagination prevented him from entrusting the young artist with any nobler task than "making a snow statue in the center of the courtyard." Such levity could hardly be tolerated by a man as deeply committed to his art as Michelangelo. His dissatisfaction became acute, and he decided to flee the court. His decision was reinforced after his sensitive nature was shaken by accounts of obscurely prophetic visions, related to him by a courtier. In October 1494, he went to Venice for a few days, then to Bologna, where news reached him of the Medicis' expulsion from Florence. A Bolognese gentleman, Gianfrancesco Aldovrandi, accorded him his protection and secured for him a commission for three statuettes for the Tomb (Arca) of San Domenico in the Basilica of San Domenico. The decoration had been begun by Nicola Pisano and his assistants Arnolfo, Fra' Guglielmo and Lapo, and continued by Niccolò—who thus acquired the name "dell'Arca"—but who did not, however, complete the work.

We can judge the importance for Michelangelo's art of his stay in Bologna from these small sculptures and many later works. He was always in the presence of the masterpieces of Jacopo della Quercia; he could contemplate, as he had done in Florence, the works of Masaccio and Giotto, and the frescoes and panels of the Ferrara masters: Tura, Cossa, Roberti. One can see, for instance, how the powerful attitude of *St Petronius* derives from Della Quercia's figures, and at the same time how the statue's vitality is enhanced by the movement of the drapery, in a subtler variation of the robes worn by Tura's Saints. *St Proculus*—described as a transition from Donatello's *St George* to Michelangelo's *David*—repeats clearly, in spite of the damage from a fall, the nervous movement in the works of Ercole de' Roberti, who, in turn, learned it from Pollaiolo. But the most beautiful statuette is the *Kneeling Angel*, a candle-bearer, twin to the one by Niccolo dell'Arca. Here we recognize, in the small, wilful, curly head, the heroes of *The Battle of Centaurs*; in the same fixed, deep gazing eyes, those of the *Madonna della Scala*. The sorrow that animates a pure Hellenistic profile is present here. The relaxed attitude of the angel's body is a consonance of classic rhythm and formidable, new plastic force. From Niccolò dell'Arca, Michelangelo accepted the suggestion of bringing to the marble "effects of a refined and minute subtlety" (Gnudi), but he converted the Bolognese's fantasy to severer, more meditative terms.

Condivi wrote: "He stayed with Messer Aldovrandi little longer than a year." Having returned to Florence near the end of 1495, Michelangelo sculptured a *Sleeping Cupid* and later a *Young St John* for Lorenzo di Pierfrancesco de' Medici. In spite of many attempts to locate them, these works, too, seem lost. We cannot visualize them except as exercises in classic art, for we know that, duly camouflaged to look like an excavated piece of antiquity, the *Cupid* was sent to Rome and sold as such to Cardinal di San Giorgio. Michelangelo was then thinking in terms of classic sculpture as we can see from the *Bacchus*, a work which he executed in Rome for the banker Jacopo Galli in 1496–97. He had gone there to assert his rights to the *Cupid* which had been sold to the Cardinal without his knowledge.

A breathtaking virtuosity is displayed in the *Bacchus*, where the classic scheme of a standing nude is made subservient to an illusionistic naturalism. The lazily moving limbs, the soft roundness of forms, which makes the marble glow with tender voluptuousness, the general insistence on psychological definition, even the furtive action of the little satyr seated on a tree-trunk behind Bacchus, convey a rich sensuality, without any trace of guilt or compunction. The moral compunction occurs later whenever Michelangelo expressed the slightest sensuality in his works. The critics have stressed the "episodic and isolated value" of this sculpture, in which they have seen "the intention to match up to the art of ancient Rome, almost as a kind of sophisticated counterfeit" (Ragghianti).

Perhaps the same sort of exhibitionism, in the guise of a revived classical form that was modified by naturalistic touches, was present in the *Cupid-Apollo* which Michelangelo also executed for Jacopo Galli. This work, too, was lost.

In 1499 Michelangelo finished the marble *Pietà*, now in

St Peter's, commissioned by Cardinal Jean Bilhères de Lagraulas.* The contract was guaranteed by Jacopo Galli, who had by now become the sculptor's friend and protector. The work was to be, Galli had promised, "more beautiful than anything in marble to be seen in Rome today, and such that no master of our own time will be able to produce better." This is evidence enough of Michelangelo's success in the humanistic circles of Rome. In this *Pietà*, his most finished sculpture (the marble is highly polished), especially in Mary's quiet restrained anguish, the critics have found elements of the clean rhythmical balance typical of Florentine tradition in the fifteenth century, traces of the designs and movement of drapery such as came originally from Ferrara, and even of Leonardo's influences. Certainly in no other sculpture was marble ever made so yielding and sensitive to light, nor was the Renaissance ideal of illusion ever fused with such an exquisite and abstract form. In the smooth surfaces of Christ's nude body and Mary's face, in contrast with the multiple refractions from the drapery, each fold of which is firmly controlled by the dominant pattern, there is an echo of Verrocchio's strongly shaded style. Verrocchio, with a goldsmith's technique, had a tendency to transform the luminous and intimate Flemish modes into complicated pictorial effects. Indeed only in Verrocchio could Michelangelo find some of the answers—insufficient and unappealing though they must have been—to the questions raised by his stay in Bologna and by his contacts with the artists of Ferrara.

Word of his success in Rome had preceded him when, perhaps in the spring of 1501, Michelangelo returned to Florence. The Republic, churches, corporations, private

*(Other sources, such as Tolnay, name Cardinal Jean de la Groslaye de Villiers.)

citizens, were all clamoring for his work. For four years, until 1505, he worked passionately and intensely, constantly striving to meet his commitments, yet searching for new means of expression. The nearest sculpture to the *Pietà*, in terms both of time and of intention, is the *Madonna and Child* now at Bruges. This highly-polished work is based upon a comparable modulation of chiaroscuro, as carried out in the contrast between the soft surfaces touched by light and the darker folds of the drapery. But the horizontal extension of the *Pietà* in Rome is replaced here by the vertical mass of the two united figures. One would not be far wrong, perhaps, in assuming that this pose may have been developed from seated figures by Nanni di Banco and early works by Donatello. There is also an ethical severity in this work, reminiscent of the *Madonna della Scala*, that is not present in the weakened sentimentality of the Rome *Pietà*. Some critics have seen in this work suggestions of Byzantine iconography and of Donatello's *Virgin of Padua*, but perhaps it is more relevant to note the continuity of classical tradition in Mary's clasping the Child's hand, a gesture similar to *Charity's* on the Pulpit by Nicola Pisano in Pisa.

In the statuettes which Michelangelo did for the Picco-lomini Altar in the Siena Cathedral (the merits of which have been so rightly vindicated by Kriegbaum), we find a strong plasticity, much like the work of the artists from Ferrara. The statuettes, representing *SS Paul*, *Peter*, *Gregory*, and *Pius*, have an architectural strength that supersedes the refined perfection of each detail. Psychological insight is marked in the extremely intelligent faces of the Saints. We find here, once again, some superb variations on the rational themes of the Ferrara masters and their abstract monumentality. Donatello's forceful yet profound rendering of individual portraits and Nanni di Banco's "primitive simplicity" are unquestionably present. Michelangelo may also have studied, for some time, the *Prophets* on Giotto's Campanile.

In 1501, Michelangelo signed the contract which meant more than anything else to him (he may have returned from Rome to Florence for just this reason), for it committed him to a task that all other contemporary artists had confessed to be beyond their powers. Michelangelo was asked to shape a figure from a huge marble block (badly roughed out forty years earlier by Agostino di Duccio) for the Office of Works of Santa Maria del Fiore. It took him eighteen months to finish the *David*. In April 1504 "the Giant," as the Florentines called it, was completed. The previous January the enthusiastic City Council had asked the greatest artists of the day, Perugino, Leonardo da Vinci, Botticelli, Filippino Lippi, Sansovino, Sangallo, and several others to form a committee to decide where the sculpture should stand. Botticelli's opinion prevailed and "the Giant" was placed in front of the Signoria Palace, as a symbol virtually of the City itself.

Tolnay has justly observed that the *David* "can be considered a synthesis of all the ideals of the Florentine Renaissance." This "super-being" embodies explicitly the classical appeal to the heroic physique. In a classic sense, the human form and its compact rhythms reflects at once universal vitality and Man's heroic consciousness and dignity. In *David's* measurements we may read the intention to exalt man. No longer is the nude an exaggeration of bodily movement or a merely descriptive exercise as in the figures of David and Hercules by Pollaiolo, Verrocchio, Bertoldo, or even Donatello. Here the extraordinary vital powers of the young hero are contained within the rhythmical ease of the stance. The quick flash of the frowning face, the turn of the wrist, the agility implied by each outline are sufficient to indicate David's tremendous power. This is the potentiality of Donatello's *St George* that gives new value to the ancient iconographical theme repeated, for instance, in the Hercules of so many sarcophagi.

The same theme had been treated before with olympic serenity by Nicola Pisano and with desperate fury by Jacopo della Quercia. The young Titan, as an "idea" of style, as a representational symbol, will reappear, with variations, in Michelangelo's paintings, the *Doni Tondo*, the *Battle of Cascina* and in some parts of the Sistine Chapel. Michelangelo carried to extreme, even outrageous, limits of articulation the innumerable poses of the human body in order to exploit all their dynamic possibilities.

The lost *David* in bronze, commissioned in 1502 by Maréchal de Rohan and finished in 1508 by Benedetto da Rovezzano, must have belonged to the same order of experiments in form.

These studies by Michelangelo of the structure of the human body were based on a representational principle clearly consonant with the Renaissance. But the terrible pressures and entanglements of his forms, the unbearable contortions, created in fact a new image of an ethical vision alien to the Renaissance spirit.

Just as he had previously absorbed and imparted a new meaning both to classic forms and to the achievements of his great Florentine predecessors, he was now trying to derive from Leonardo's work all that was relevant to his problems and to his artistic intentions. The two artists were both engaged in preparing the designs for the decoration of the new Council Hall in the Palazzo Vecchio. Leonardo expressed his vision of cosmic unity by drawing into "the center of action the warriors of the *Battle of Anghiari* and Nature itself." Michelangelo, on the other hand, in the

Battle of Cascina, conceived of the universal forces as being contained in Man, and expressed through his physique. For Leonardo, Man consciously adapts himself to natural forces. By blurring the lines between figures and background, by handling paint as a unifying medium (*sfumato*), and by posing his figures in natural attitudes, Leonardo recreates a harmonious world. But for Michelangelo Man is the central, isolated agent, sharply defined in empty space. His powerful body and its excessive straining toward expression (*contrapposto*) claim the world's energies for himself.

The essential difference between the two artists should be considered in examining Michelangelo's two sculptures, executed between 1503 and 1506, which have been frequently cited as imitative of Leonardo's work. These are *The Pitti Madonna*, now at the Bargello Museum, and *The Taddei Madonna* at the Royal Academy in London. In the Bargello sculpture, true, Leonardo's influence can be seen in the composition of the Child's figure, and in the softening of form where, by scraping the surfaces, Michelangelo made them more sensitive to light. In other words, the imputation is valid only for a general "effect" that is secondary to the basic idea—Michelangelo's alone—of expressing, even in a familiar religious image, a rigorous moral consciousness reinforced by substantial form.

The Virgin in the Bargello is similar, in a way, to the *Madonna della Scala*, but freed of the archaic severity imposed by the shallow relief. She appears, in fact, in a natural attitude, the space about her made less abstract by the block on which she sits. She holds between her knees the Child whose curved pose repeats the tondo's circular border. But the turn of Mary's head breaks the circle; and the bend of the head and arm of Jesus emphasize his *contrapposto*.

Leonardo's influence is more marked in the London

bas-relief, in the straining reach, for instance of the Child, taken obviously from a known Leonardo motif that appears in his drawings, from *The Madonna of the Cat* to the *St Anne, Virgin and Child*, and notably the small Cupids in *Leda*. A more subtle but none the less clear reflection of Leonardo is the handling of space as "atmosphere." The composition of *The Pitti Madonna* directs each element to the central axis of Mary's figure and derives dramatic interest from the severe and intent look in her eyes. Here, however, the figures move away from the center, where the sheer emptiness of the space is heightened by the little bird fluttering in the grasp of St John. But even this bas-relief, close as it is to certain of Leonardo's techniques, is unquestionably Michelangelo's. If he did not refine every part, it was not just to accent the contrast of light and shadow. The slow movement of Mary's head, her throat, her hand clutching the drapery and the Child's energetic turn (the figure is almost a high-relief) stand out from the roughed-in surface as focal points of the felt life in this composition.

This "roughing-in" or incompleteness occurs frequently in Michelangelo's work. In fact his unfinished works (unfinished, that is, in a technical sense only) are more numerous than his finished ones. And we must take into account that those of an architectural-sculptural nature were reduced, in terms of complexity and dimension, from his original plans, if not abandoned altogether, while all his great pictorial cycles were finished in every sense of the word. Vasari himself noticed that the number of "unfinished statues is far greater," and felt that any material explanation of this (the scarcity of marble, for instance, or too many commitments, complaints from patrons, or obstacles put in the master's way by jealous colleagues) would in the end be inadequate. He sought, therefore, a deeper reason for the unfinished works, and found it in Michelangelo's continual dissatisfaction. Cellini put forward another explanation, in connexion with the famous dispute over the merits of sculpture and painting: "The great Michelangelo has painted about a thousand pictures for each piece of sculpture that he has carved, for painting is so much easier, and is not exposed on so many sides." The critical problem of "incompleteness" was thus posed, for the first time, even if imprecisely, in its double aspect of psychology and representation. It was to emerge again in modern criticism, as central to the interpretation of Michelangelo's art, with the writings of Guillaume and, later, of Justi and Thode.

We shall not rehearse this dispute here, but it may be interesting to recall Aru's recapitulation of the various opinions in the introduction to his own theory: "Some have claimed that a condition of permanent dissatisfaction prevented Michelangelo from finishing what he had set out to do and caused him to leave his work incompleted, either because the external conflict between spirit and matter left him tragically shaken (Mariani), or because he found it impossible to infuse a Christian mystical content into a pagan form (Thode). Others have believed, conversely, that he suddenly abandoned his work because he was satisfied that he had duly represented his vision: because incompleteness gives an added plastic freshness to a subject (Venturi, Bertini); because a greater pathos can be expressed by a quick bold synthesis (Bertini); because a form striving to escape from a block stresses its own movement (Bertini); out of love for ancient sculptures which appear more powerful and expressive for being corroded or truncated (Toesca); or finally because figures emerging from rough marble give the impression that the human spirit is mingling with natural forces, thereby taking advantage of an abstraction, as against the limitations of precisely located or defined personality (Bettini)." Aru, for his part, recalled Cellini's words about Michelangelo needing "an imperative unity of vision," as confirmed by his method of "*extracting* his figures from the marble by means of his chisel" (Vasari), meaning that he actually conceived sculpture in terms of "taking out." Michelangelo, therefore, stopped working at the precise moment when the creation of new surfaces might have marred the artistic excellence of his work, for sculpture "goes on evolving, little by little." This is a very shrewd remark, and it also helps us to understand why Michelangelo found painting—technically a single surface—a medium in which he could more readily express his vision.

It is always true that when one tries to explain why an artist chose one form and not another, or rather why his finished artistic product turned out to be different from his statement of poetic intentions, the man's original motive can only be conjectured. On the other hand, there is no such thing as an abstract "Nature," just as there is no abstract "incompleteness"; the artistic finality, for instance, of Michelangelo's *Moses* is a totally different thing from the technical refinement of the *Pietà* in St Peter's. Similarly the deliberate lack of polish and finish, in *The Pitti Madonna* or in the *David-Apollo*, that diffuses the light on their surfaces is different from the Leonardo-like blurring of *The Taddei Madonna* and even more from the indefiniteness—as Aru says "to achieve psychological expression"—of the heads of *Dusk* and *Day* in the Medici Chapel or of the *Pietà* in the Duomo at Florence. In the *St Matthew*, or in the *Captives*, also at Florence, what is unfinished is not only the treatment of the surfaces or the naturalistic rendering of some details, but the very composition of the image in its essence. This means that every work should be judged on its own merits in the light of artistic intention, and with an eye toward the place it occupies in the chronology of Michelangelo's activity.

If we take an historical view of this "incompleteness" we shall observe, to begin with, that the first works to which—appropriately or not—that term could be applied belong to the period of Michelangelo's early undertakings, such as the *Battle of Cascina*, the Tomb of Julius II, the ceiling of the Sistine Chapel, which was also the period when his meditations upon Man's heroic dignity found new scope. His severe but still serene conception of humanity controlling its own destiny was being modified, through the artist's own suffering, by the recognition that like the world around him he too obeyed divine Necessity. He was conscious of being the center of the world, but not the world's creator. Man is, in fact, a being created from matter and forever burdened with its weight. The artist's highest aim was now to express this dramatic consciousness in the enclosed, tortuous rhythm of absolute form. But this form could no longer remain bound to the conventions of the Renaissance, however daring or violent they may have been. That fundamental respect for a classic canon which was basic to the creations of fifteenth-century sculptors was definitely abandoned: Michelangelo's "hazardous dream," as Longhi remarked, had to be enacted, representationally, by a deviation from the classic conception of form. His new expression would consist of human symbols whose standard of beauty would be found in the relationship between their deformed sizes and exaggerated gestures and Michelangelo's own tormented moral vision. In Longhi's words, this concept meant: "A titan race of fettered slaves, of high-waisted Sibyls, of unforgettable elders." It should be clear, now, that the scraped surfaces, the Leonardo-like softening and psychological indefiniteness are no more than secondary elements of the whole inventive complex in which they appear. Thus the incompleteness of such compositions as *St Matthew*, the *Captives* at Florence, and the *Rondanini Pietà* is part of the meaning of the presented image. And because, in these cases as well, we are confronted with works which are aesthetic wholes, we need not speculate on Michelangelo's original intentions. In each of these masterpieces the composition confirms the artist's best style: he could well have worked at his marble block until he developed in all its implications the theme which he had undertaken to express, or equally he could have stopped because the tension between form and matter is the best artistic means to embody what Briganti called "his mighty feeling for the irreconcilable."

Let us now examine Michelangelo's first unfinished work, the *St Matthew*. This is the only one of twelve figures of the Apostles commissioned in 1503 for Santa Maria del Fiore that Michelangelo executed. He did not carry out the full commitment because he was suddenly summoned to Rome in March 1505, by Pope Julius II who entrusted him with the design of his own tomb. It is possible that the Pontiff's choice was due to the advice of Giuliano da Sangallo. The monument was designed and the necessary marbles excavated and shipped; Michelangelo wrote to Fantoni some years later that the sculpture had been "roughed out." Work progressed probably well in to 1506, when the Pope appeared to have changed his mind. Incensed, Michelangelo returned to Florence.

This unfinished *St Matthew*, undoubtedly one of the master's most sublime conceptions, announces Man's heroic confidence—as Mariani so aptly described it—as do the *David* and the drawings for the *Battle of Cascina*. But the serene energy of those nudes gave place, here, to a passionate and primitive sense of power. Classic harmony of "beautiful limbs" was abandoned in favor of a fury of conflicting gestures: the lightning movement of the Saint's head; the sharp profile which was to reappear in the *Eternal Father* on the vaulting of the Sistine Chapel; the enormous eye, fixed on the divine apparition; the twisted shoulder; the left leg desperately pushing against the block as if it were forcing the figure out of the marble; all this tortured collision between masses is given an added pathos by the chiselled surfaces and the roughed-out forms. In this titanic defender of the faith, Michelangelo expressed his own inner torment and did so in a daring composition, for only he had the assurance and the spiritual energy to carry off such a *tour de force*.

We may well imagine, therefore, how Michelangelo must have envisioned the Tomb of Julius II. Perhaps as a triumphant chronicle of Man's struggle to achieve peace by means of Faith. He had visualized an "imposing, purifying pyramid" (de Tolnay), somewhat like ancient mausoleums, but here, as in his sculptures, he would re-create classical motifs with a revolutionary Christian vigor. The architectural grandeur of the design is conveyed to us by the descriptions —superficial and contradictory though they are—of Condivi and Vasari (see plans on page 58): a four-sided tabernacle, approximately 30 feet long and 20 feet wide, and inside it the Papal tomb, the whole structure free-standing in the transept of the Basilica. The impact would have been powerful: the *Slaves* struggling against their bonds, the *Victories* vital and brilliant, and the *Sibyls* and *Prophets* brooding on human experience and divine revelation, and finally the elevated figure of the Pope, upheld by allegorical *Heaven* and *Earth*. In this glorification of one individual, the history of humanity would have been celebrated; everything was to be expressed through human forms as an anthropocentric rite. This was Michelangelo's boldest dream; to enfold what is infinite, eternal, universal, within an articulate, well-defined structure that Man can apprehend. The realization of this dream tormented him all his life and one can well understand that the "tragedy of the sepulchral monument" was due not only to external obstacles that prevented his finishing the task but also, indeed mainly, to his passionate need for carrying out in every detail, with no compromise, what he had set out to do. He chose, in the end, to abandon this whole scheme and, instead, executed the present Tomb (in the Church of San Pietro in Vincoli) which, though noble, is a considerable scaling down of his original idea. Michelangelo was then compelled, in place of one monumental effort, to fragment his vision, in single sculptures, such as the *Captives*, or in larger projects, like the Medici Chapel, St Peter's, and the Sistine Chapel ceiling.

The first plan for the Tomb was discarded after a whole year of preparation. In 1505, when Pope Julius approved it, Michelangelo went to Carrara where he remained eight months to choose the marbles and supervise their excavation. On his return to Rome he found that the Pope had changed his mind; he had abandoned the scheme for a new dais planned by Rossellino in St Peter's (on which the Tomb was to be erected) in favor of a new design for the whole Basilica submitted by Bramante. Michelangelo's rivals had not wasted their time; the Pontiff would not even see him.

Anger and frustration drove him to return to Florence the day before the foundation-stone was laid for Bramante's Basilica. Back in his own city he worked furiously on the *Battle of Cascina*, on the *St Matthew*, and perhaps on the reliefs of the *Madonna*. He resisted the Pope's pleas and threats until, on the advice of many friends, he decided in November 1506, even though unrepentant, to accede to Julius, who was at Bologna. The reconciliation was sealed by the commission for a great bronze statue of the Pope to be placed on the façade of the Church of St Petronius. This work took a long time because Michelangelo had little experience with bronze. Finally, in February 1508, the statue was placed upon the Church's façade, but it was destroyed three years later by the populace celebrating the Bentivoglios' return. Unfortunately no drawings or copies of it have survived.

In March 1508, Michelangelo was in Florence, and April found him in Rome where on May 10 he signed a contract for the frescoes of the Sistine Chapel ceiling. This was to mean four years of terrifying work for him, but he created a vast and coherent spectacle. Here we find a history of the spirit in the awesome range of human and divine figures. This is what Michelangelo had dreamed, perhaps, of achieving in the Tomb of Julius II. In the frescoes, as in the Tomb, the architecture and the figures are indissolubly connected by lines of extraordinary energy. The whole is permeated with endless movement, but still governed everywhere by a rational order.

Later, in *The Dying Slave* (the Louvre) we shall recognize the development of a motif that Michelangelo had originally conceived in the *Nude* on the right of the *Libyan Sibyl*.

This sculpture, and the other one called *The Rebellious Slave*, were carved in 1513 when, after the death of Julius II, Michelangelo signed a new contract for the Tomb with the Pope's heirs. At the Ashmolean Museum, Oxford, are six sketches of captives, dated 1512–13: one of them is undoubtedly related to *The Rebellious Slave* in the Louvre. In these two figures, Michelangelo seems to go back to Da Vinci's easy *contrapposto*, with which he had previously experimented in the *Doni Tondo*, in *St Matthew*, in the *Battle of Cascina* and on the Sistine Chapel ceiling. But Leonardo's fluidity of movement is arrested, here and in Michelangelo's other works, by one gesture which, involving the whole body in the most strenuous tension, compels it to full articulation and reveals its potential. Each action is thus enlarged and made heroic by the strain to which the body is subjected, and the strain itself is measured by each rippling muscle and tendon of these titanic figures who struggle against the bonds of their own physical weight. *The Dying Slave*'s youthful body is developed along a sinuous line going from the elbow thrust upward to the hip; he seems to be sliding into space with an almost sensuous abandon reflected in his beautiful, dreamy face. His right hand has stopped tugging at the strap around his chest; only his legs are still making a last, feeble effort. This form and its pathos recall once again the Hellenistic marbles, and we understand how it later inspired the Mannerists, removed though they were from its moral severity, as a new canon of formal beauty and an example for their uneasy but attenuated spiritual attitudes.

The Dying Slave has succumbed and will fight no longer, but *The Rebellious Slave* is still desperately straining at his bonds, his head raised to the sky either in supplication or in defiance. Here, too, the dynamic violence of the sculpture is expressed through *contrapposto* in the pose: as the muscular shoulder is projected forward the head strains upward; the torso moves in one direction, the right leg in the opposite one. By the unrestrained muscularity of the image, freedom and rebellion are represented concretely.

Between 1513 and 1516 Michelangelo sculptured the *Moses*. This was the only statue of the many he had conceived and executed for the Tomb actually to find a place in the final project. Comparable in grandeur and spiritual energy to the figures on the Sistine Chapel ceiling, *Moses*, even within

the restraint of a seated pose, reveals immediately his super-
natural powers. The essential figure, the same as the *Prophet
Joel's*, was to be repeated, with variations, in the statue of
Giuliano de' Medici. He is ready for action: the left foot is
pressing backward and the tension is increased by a sudden
turn of the head and then counter-balanced by the arm
brought forward and by the flow of the beard. Light runs
along the smooth surfaces and vibrates in the pleats of the
robe, in the Prophet's muscles, in the hairs of his beard; we
have thus a sense of continuing movement controlled by the
massive composition. The Prophet's holy wrath is symbolic
once again of Michelangelo's worship of Man, that no longer
serves a classical ideal of balance, or naturalistic conventions,
but rather the artist's tormented moral consciousness.

Michelangelo was probably still working on the *Moses*
when he signed the third contract for the Tomb of Julius II
in July 1516. His plans for the monument were changed
once more; the scale was reduced and so was the number of
decorative sculptures. But, as always, new commitments
prevented him from executing the task. This time Pope
Leo X—who admired and befriended Michelangelo to the
point of making him a Palatine Count—entrusted him with
the façade of the Church of San Lorenzo in Florence. From
1516 to 1520 the artist moved continuously between Rome,
Carrara, Florence, and Pietrasanta (where he chose the
marble for the façade). He even made a model and started
chiselling the marble, but in March 1520 the Pope cancelled
the contract, offending Michelangelo deeply. The only
sculptures he executed in those years were the two versions
of the *Risen Christ*, commissioned in 1514 for the Church of
Santa Maria sopra Minerva in Rome. The first version,
which was begun that year and not finished because of the
lack of marble, has been lost. The second one, though

lessened in quality by the continual changes, retains a distinct formal harmony. The classic nude is conceived in a quiet spiral of rhythms, and the tender expression of the face, turned toward the viewer, is the artist's only concession to conventional iconography, for in this work too, Michelangelo strove to impart a Christian meaning to a pagan form.

In the same period another great project failed to develop. In October 1519, Michelangelo suggested to the Pope that he should honor the poet Dante by erecting a monument to him in Florence. The sculptor had always been an admirer and an avid reader of Dante's, as shown not only by his sculptures and paintings but by his sonnets dedicated to the poet and in a "conversation" of Donato Giannotti. But nothing came of the suggestion.

The master stayed in Florence, working on the sculptures for the Tomb of Julius II. He refused the invitation of his friends, especially Sebastiano del Piombo, to go back to Rome where the Vatican doors were open to him now that Raphael was dead. In the meantime he was repeatedly asked by Giulio de' Medici, who later became Pope Clement VII, and by Leo X, to design a chapel in San Lorenzo for the tombs of Lorenzo the Magnificent, of his brother Giuliano, of Lorenzo Duke of Urbino, and of Giuliano Duke of Nemours. Having at first refused, Michelangelo accepted the offer in November 1520, and promised that he would also finish the Tomb of Julius II. In 1524, while he was working on the Chapel, Clement VII entrusted him with the planning of the Biblioteca Laurenziana (Laurentian Library). From that year to 1536—when he settled permanently in Rome and began to paint the *Last Judgment* in the Sistine Chapel, by order of Paul III—Michelangelo was very productive. He travelled constantly from Rome to Florence and back, working alternately on the Tomb—for which he produced two new plans in 1526 and in 1532 for Julius II's heirs who were reproaching and threatening him for the delay—on the Medici Chapel, on the Biblioteca, and on a canopy and a raised stand for relics in the Church of San Lorenzo.

In 1527, before the sack of Rome, Michelangelo had gone to Florence where, after the expulsion of the Medici, he had been entrusted with the city's fortifications. He travelled to Ferrara to study its famous bastions and received a commission for a painting from Duke Alfonso d'Este, for whom he later drew the *Leda*. In September 1529, anticipating Malatesta Baglioni's betrayal, he fled to Ferrara again and then to Venice. The Republic of Florence proclaimed him a traitor, but he was soon exonerated and he returned to the city during a siege in which he is said to have acted courageously. When Florence capitulated, he went into hiding in the Tower of St Nicholas, but later the Pope pardoned him and he was able to resume work on the Medici Chapel.

Besides these sculptures he executed, in those years, the *David-Apollo*, the drawings for *Noli Me Tangere* and for *Venus and Cupid*, *The Victory* in the Signoria Palace at Florence, perhaps the *Captives* (Accademia), and a series of mythological drawings for Tommaso Cavalieri, a very handsome and cultivated Roman youth whose friendship Michelangelo prized.

A few years earlier, possibly in 1528, he had executed a clay model of *Hercules and Cacus* (Casa Buonarroti). In the powerful spiral of the two bodies locked in combat we see once again the heroic and despairing motif of Man's eternal struggle. The tremendous contortions and elaborate composition create an intense drama, the vitality of which was not understood by Michelangelo's admirers and followers, who attempted his monumentality but with rather cold, academic results or sought for intellectual elegance and an elaborate virtuosity of form which they were not up to. Even the greatest of them, those whose style comes out of some moral concern, failed to grasp the essence of his art, for their works betray a certain unrelieved complacency.

Michelangelo's power as an allegorist is unquestionably realized in the Medici Chapel where the relationship between Man and Eternity takes form in both the stark architecture and expressive sculptures. In the exactitude and severity of this defined area, regulated by the norm of "divine proportions," there is an obvious echo of Brunelleschi, though the latter's limpid serenity and the simplicity with which he used space give way here to a more solemn austerity in the structure and ornament. This Chapel is a product of heroic sensibility, as it brings back to life the fundamentals of Roman classicism within a lucid perspective that is distinctly Renaissance. Again, Michelangelo attempted to contain within a coherent form Man's vacillation between impulse and necessity, between rebellion and judgment. The severe architecture that directs the energetic movement of the stone framework and ceiling compartments, of the marble ledges and scrolls, provides an appropriate background for the figures above the tombs. The young heroes turn to Mary, as if they recognize in her the greatest example of sorrowful but serene acceptance of fate.

These figures, though being absolutely "invented" by representational standards, are correlated to one another and to the chapel's architecture by the consistent composition. But at the same time they are perfectly independent as organic units; they have a vital, formidable physical immediacy; each one of them seems activated by his own impulses. They react perfectly to the restrained environment: the Chapel is built around them, commensurate to their size and to the dramatic implications of their attitudes: the solitary torment of the great allegories of Time, Lorenzo's absorption, Giuliano's readiness. Across the Chapel from the Tombs, between the Saints by Montorsoli and Raffaello da Montelupo, the Madonna seems lost in the same absorption while in the very act of satisfying the Child's thirst for life.

In the case of the Chapel, too, Michelangelo prepared many designs before making his final choice that upset so many conventions. He had planned many more sculptures and frescoes. Two of the excluded statues still exist: the model for a *River Divinity* in the Accademia in Florence, whose athletic but weary body vainly strives to overcome its own physical weight. Like the *Belvedere* this is one more example of Hellenistic art which Michelangelo was constantly trying to interpret and repeat. The second sculpture is the *Crouching Youth* (Leningrad), another "thorn remover" reduced to a single knot of pulsating, distended muscles. Michelangelo attempted, apparently, every pose which constricts and strains the human body in order to dramatize the potential energy that is trapped in it.

The anguished titanic figures of the Medici Chapel express their blind revolt against superior forces in an altogether distinctive plastic idiom. Instead of the convulsed, compact masses of *Hercules and Cacus*, the *River Divinity* and the *Crouching Youth*, the images here are freer, more open; they are elongated, their outlines more elliptic; their movement is admittedly still complicated and twisted, but modified by the play of light on the more exposed surfaces. What we have here, in fact, is a superb example of *contrapposto* as originally applied in the *Doni Tondo* and in the frescoes of the Sistine Chapel ceiling. This is the reason why many critics have traced relationships with the Mannerists and Tolnay has written that "the excess of forces would appear to be exhausted; the artist is looking at the spectacle from a distance." The very composition of each tomb—an apparent pyramid mitigated by the many diverging lines running through it—reveals a complicated rhythmical pattern; repetition of line on the one hand, and on the other, diverging focal points in the individual figures. At the same time, however, the subtle, rational dialectic of forces is secondary to the gravity and immediacy of the theme. Our pre-occupation with the feeling of the Chapel as a whole causes us to forget the techniques and historical refrains that make up the effect. Lorenzo's elaborate pose enables a play of light and dark over the ample surfaces: a slow wave softly enfolds his great body, starting from the helmet and casting a shadow over his fine, absorbed features. And underneath this brooding figure we see the beautiful allegories of *Dusk*, his head disconsolately bent over his powerful, relaxed chest, and of *Dawn*, a young divinity in an agonized awakening. But the statue of Giuliano, in contrast to Lorenzo, is governed by anticipation. Reclining on his sarcophagus, *Night* and *Day* follow the canon of *contrapposto*: they are two Titans gripped in the tension of muscles and limbs. *Night* seems to be yearning for sleep and illusion:

> Sleep is dear to me, but being stone dearer
> So long as this hurt and shame shall last;
> Not to see, not to hear would be my fortune.
> Do not awaken me: speak in a whisper.

These few lines by Michelangelo are the most appropriate comment on the figure of *Night*. *Day*, a disdainful giant, has an almost accusing expression on his angry face.

The most moving of these masterpieces is the *Madonna and Child*. She is detached from the visible emotions of the allegorical figures, so absorbed in her sorrow as to appear unconscious of her very actions. Here Michelangelo returned to the conception of his youth, the *Madonna of the Stairs*, but with a greater sense of life and more articulation. Mary distractedly feeds the Christ Child but she is absorbed in the feeling that dominates the Chapel: the life-giving act is counter-balanced by the brooding tone. Again a composition bordering on Mannerism (the sinuous figure, the spiralling group) is a powerful metaphor for the ambiguous presence in common reality of uncommon forces.

In other works, the location and date of which are difficult to establish with any certainty, but which were probably done between 1525 and 1535, the master revealed how a single formula or mode can be applied to several themes. His *David-Apollo*, it has been said, seems almost an echo of *The Risen Christ* in Santa Maria sopra Minerva. A careful examination of the two sculptures, however, shows notable differences which hardly need mentioning. This dreamy Apollo, turning languidly with a half-gesture, softly lighted over the opaque surfaces, seems to derive a sensuous pleasure from the knowledge of his own beauty. In *The Victory* in the Signoria Palace, however, we find the same spiral grouping of two figures that we have seen in the model for *Hercules and Cacus*, but shaped with entirely different artistic intentions. While the model is a group of masses projected downwards, here the youth, indifferent to the giant barbarian he has conquered and who silently rages at the humiliation of being turned into a pedestal, unfolds his nervous, elegant body in an upward movement. As those in the Medici Chapel, these figures are not classically or anatomically proportioned, but their measurements obey only the rules of dynamic rhythm as they become longer or shorter in a series of calculated, and incredibly fluid distortions. The dramatic contrast between the silent fury of the vanquished barbarian and the young victor's beautiful, dispassionate face heightens the visual experience. This sculpture may have been intended for the fifth project of the Tomb of Julius II, drawn up in 1532.

A short time later perhaps, Michelangelo roughed out the splendid four *Slaves* or *Captives* (Accademia, Florence), though several critics have dated them earlier. It seems hardly possible to hazard a comment on these four monumental representations of despair and revolt. In the Medici Chapel, the allegories of Time express the torment caused by sorrow and vain aspirations, and the other figures in counterpoint, express the triumph of Stoicism. A comparable moral infuses the *Captives* who symbolize, in the allegory of the Tomb, the moment of uncontrolled passion, the blind fury of those who, lacking faith (that is to say, reason), will not accept their condition, but only submit to it in exhaustion. The *Youthful Captive* seems to be weeping—sobs are shaking his strong but useless frame; the *Bearded Captive* has given up struggling and passively submits to his future of serfdom; *Atlas* bears on his shoulders the enormous weight placed there by his new masters but he still struggles; the last one, the *Awakening Captive*, twists his body spasmodically, pushing against the stone that imprisons him, and turns his head to the sky, shouting a protest and a prayer.

As we have already said, the meaning of these figures, in terms of composition, is fully understandable even in their incompleteness. But such is the moving contrast between form and substance, such is the visual power of this image of man painfully emerging from matter that always weighs him down, that we may well ask if, by so presenting his works, Michelangelo did not consciously create an early Expressionism. In recalling the Medici Chapel statues and the various versions of the *Pietà*, we cannot answer the question, with any finality, whether the simultaneous presence in those works of polished areas and roughed-in patches indicates deliberate artistic intention or not. The fact remains that in these *Slaves* we have found Michelangelo's poetry exemplified:

> There is no concept in the mind of an excellent artist
> that one piece of marble may not contain
> in its abundance, and that is reached
> only by the hand which obeys the Mind.

If we now look at the *Slaves* (Louvre) and at the sculptures of the decade preceding the *Captives* (Florence), we observe how the compact and facile modeling, the nervous plastic flexibility of that period has been replaced, in the *Captives*, by an expansion of heavy masses, of large rough surfaces, whose latent force is suddenly revealed by sharp outlines cut in the block with a few violent strokes. "Clearly," Carli writes, "Michelangelo was moving towards the last phase of his art, in which the progressive internalization of his forms requires only a few essential strokes to exact from the broken stone pure signs of spirit." This then may also be the moral burden of the great frescoes: the *Last Judgment* and the *Stories of SS Peter and Paul* in the Sistine and Pauline Chapels; and the drawings which Michelangelo did for Tommaso Cavalieri and Vittoria Colonna, the woman whom he loved and who guided and comforted him during his moral crises.

It would be out of context here to discuss all Michelangelo's activities during his last years in Rome, when he finished masterpieces like the Vatican frescoes and St Peter's. But the sculptures of this period have a particular interest, for they enable us to follow more closely his spiritual life.

When he finished his great pictorial cycles and once he felt free of commitments to the heirs of Julius II, Michelangelo concentrated on official architectural enterprises in order to attempt large images that would express universal order. Privately he continued his sculpture as a form of confessional and therapy for his increasing disquiet. When still in Florence he had planned a *Colossus* for the Piazza di San Lorenzo, and Clement VII encouraged him. The enormous figure would have functioned as the church tower "and the sound of bells shall come out of his mouth, so that he will appear to be shouting *misericordia*, especially on holidays when the bigger bells will ring often." The urge for gigantic feats was gnawing at him, as when, some time before, he had thought of carving a statue directly out of a mountain in the Apuan Alps. But this urge was now dimmed by the anguish which eventually motivated his Roman frescoes.

In Rome, shortly after 1538, he did a bust of *Brutus* for his friend Donato Giannotti. Imperial Roman busts are seldom more than superficial. Michelangelo, however, rendered this portrait with an absolute severity that rejects all rhetoric or pathos: a small compact head, its features firmly and tensely carved, and the rough and vague classic profile, are all we need to feel the righteousness of the tyrannicide. The scraped surfaces, catching a softer light, impart life and character to the idealized mask.

Not before 1545 did Michelangelo complete the work that had been his frustration: the Tomb of Julius II. But how different it was from the image he had originally conceived! The monument we now see in San Pietro in Vincoli, which was to have been his greatest glory, the summation of Man's triumphs and defeats, his sorrows and dignity, is but a shadow of the master's first ambitious projects. It is a desperate compromise which he accepted in order to have done with threats and slanders, for the Pope's heirs even accused him, among other things, of embezzlement. "I have wasted my youth tied to this Sepulchre!" he wrote ironically, in defense of his work. The architecture of the Tomb is powerful, none the less, with its hard framework and the clarity of juxtaposed masses and spaces. Looking at it from the side, one can fully appreciate the value of this chastened structure, the composition of which becomes simpler at the top, where the eye is led by the upward expansion of the smooth pillars. But mediocre statues, done by assistants, detract from the whole frame, and the design is precisely intended to frame the statue of *Moses*. The figures of *Leah* and *Rachel*, though, are certainly by Michelangelo; indeed they mark an important moment in his development. Some critics have described them as cold, academic works, attributable to the master's assistants, but they really are much more: studies, as it were, in coherent, novel form. Michelangelo's pupils collaborated only partially in the finishing, and certainly their overall merit has not suffered. Of course one should not look to these figures for the impetus or for the plasticity visible in so many other works, but rather we can see a quiescence and serene confidence expressed by their slow, undulating postures, consonant with their roles as Faith and Charity. In *Leah* and *Rachel* we find examples of Michelangelo's search for severer and chastened forms. This search is further documented by Michelangelo's drawings of that period. It is as if he were transposing his austere religious principles in poetic form; his former urge toward the "titanic" now placated by mystical contemplations.

Michelangelo's religious anxiety, his obsessive brooding on salvation, was nourished by the reformers who gathered round Vittoria Colonna. But one cannot imagine Michelangelo following any one particular doctrine: his was a solitary dialogue with his own conscience. He now expressed through architecture his conviction that man, having admitted the necessity of his condition, can shape form and space into a microcosm of universal order. In his statues, done for the most part in secret, Michelangelo turned more and more to the Passion of Christ and His Crucifixion.

From 1545 to his death in 1564—besides a bas-relief for Vittoria Colonna of which only copies have survived—Michelangelo worked on three different groups of the *Pietà*, through which we may follow the last developments of his artistic ideal and his style. The first one, in chronological order, appears to have been the *Palestrina Pietà*, though the authenticity of this work is still under discussion. On the one hand, the treatment of surfaces, less vibrant than in the master's documented sculptures, and the unusual softness of some areas, and, on the other hand, total lack of references to it even in the oldest biographies, partially justify the doubts of some scholars. One should bear in mind, however, that when it was moved into the Chapel of the Barberini Palace at Palestrina, the group was covered, in the typical bad taste of the Baroque, with a heavy coating of plaster, perhaps to conceal the unfinished parts or to alter it according to the seventeenth-century notion of chiaroscuro. Here, surely, the pathos is so extreme, it is almost forced. One may trace the origins of the expanded form, the enormous inert masses, in the broad modeling of the Florence *Captives*, but their restrained vigor has been replaced, in this *Pietà*, by an inert heaviness. The similarity between these figures and the torpid giants in the *Last Judgment*, or in the Pauline Chapel, is proof that we are confronted here with a work which Michelangelo could have conceived only in these last years. Christ's huge nerveless body crumples downwards as Mary hugs it to her breast, desperately watching His face; Mary Magdalen bends in the effort to hold up the dead Savior. The large torso of Jesus is the focal point of the total movement, a definite *contrapposto*: the collapse of the head and arm against the upward straining of the Magdalen, and the falling body pressing against the indomitable figure of the Virgin.

Contrasting with these tortured images, other sculptures, inspired by serener faith, show a return of the vitality typical of Michelangelo's maturity, but more restrained. The splendid *Pietà* in the Duomo in Florence, datable between 1547 and 1555, although a gnarl of opposed movements, has a persuasive effect of tenderness and harmony. Here, Nicodemus may be Michelangelo himself, helping and watching over Mary. The group, from the front, is very wide, though it does not offer the viewer the massive square appearance of the *Palestrina Pietà*; it is rather a complex of starts and fragmentations. From the apex of Nicodemus's hood, the visual focus moves downwards, and as it broadens it breaks into a hundred dramatic contrasts of lean, elongated forms, interrupted by sudden breaks in the outlines, and eventually settling at the base of the pyramid, with a minor reprise in the cavity created by Christ's folded leg. The movement of the falling body crumpling backwards into Mary's arms is broken twice, in opposite directions, the fractured spiral increasing the pathos. Therefore, by complicating the visual means with his own formula ("the figure should be pyramidal, serpentine and multiplied by one, by two and by three") Michelangelo seems to have gone back, beyond Donatello, to the Gothic idioms of Giovanni Pisano's final period, when his vigorous, compact forms became softer and more flexible.

Michelangelo's passion and diligence as he worked this sculpture is noted by Vasari who, in explaining the technical reasons why Michelangelo broke the statue and finally abandoned it ("the marble had too much foreign material, it was too hard, it was marred by a vein"), could not help adding, "or it could have been that the man's critical faculties were so great that he was never pleased with what he had done." Michelangelo was already thinking of a new version of a *Pietà* and could no longer bear to work at a sculpture the "concept" of which had been completely expressed. "He had grown to hate it," Vasari writes, "and having lost his patience he broke it; he wanted to break it up altogether but his friends took it away because it was precious."

Three drawings kept at Oxford record Michelangelo's first ideas for the *Rondanini Pietà*. The group is reduced just to the figures of Mary and Jesus, thus restricting the drama to its essential elements. The forms are large, expanded, and suspended in light which appears to emanate from within them; the physical tension between the collapsing weight of Christ's body and the Virgin's effort to sustain him implies spiritual tension. The master began working on this group shortly before 1553, but soon abandoned it, as if its realization had deprived his vision of its value. He went back to it in the last year of his life. While his friends believed that he was carrying on day by day out of sheer habit ("it became necessary to provide him with pieces of marble so that he could spend part of each day with his hammer and chisel"), Michelangelo was actually creating new forms.

In the first version, as the drawings and the remaining arm seem to prove, Jesus was slim but powerful; He fell forward, with His head and chest framed by the graceful line of the shroud; the Virgin, with her arms around Him, looked imploringly up at the heavens. This, however, was an image of passion, grave but still passion, and the forms stood out too clearly. An excess of physical definitions was employed to express a feeling which transcended the struggle against matter, and had become a pure desire for salvation.

At that point, Michelangelo destroyed what he had done and started again. He eventually succeeded in extracting from the very same block of marble a totally new conception. The two slight, superimposed figures move in a wide ascending curve; they are indissolubly united and have become one body. Not only does the mother hold her Son to her breast, but He appears to be still alive. Perhaps it is not absurd to surmise that, in elaborating the sculpture, Michelangelo left Christ's legs untouched so that, from these well-defined naturalistic limbs, our eyes may rise to other forms whose plastic values are to be found in their very lack of definition and detail. They are rendered by only layers of light and dark, as if in search of transcendence. But assuming that we have been deceived by the incompleteness into attributing to it a stylistic intention, it is clear that the sculptor intended here to make his marble as sensitive to light as he possibly could: clearly articulated surfaces and outlines are replaced by a diffused, vague luminosity. Mere physical beauty was being abandoned for purer feeling. Michelangelo's departure from classicism had reached its most extreme point. Between the smooth and sentimental perfection of the *Pietà* in St Peter's to these consumed, phantom figures, there is an enormous difference in plastic means, but a striking coherence in artistic intention.

The "excellent artist" had now succeeded in expressing even the inexpressible in sculpture.

In February 1564, Michelangelo, though exhausted by his long illness, was still working on the *Rondanini* group in the house of Macel de' Corvi, in Rome.

And thus, still creating, and bequeathing to humanity the most moving image of that "Divine Love" to which his soul was now entirely dedicated, Michelangelo died, on February 18, 1564.

BIOGRAPHICAL NOTES

1475, MARCH 6. Michelangelo Buonarroti is born in Caprese, in the border area between Tuscany and Umbria, the son of Lodovico di Lionardo di Buonarroto Simoni, Mayor of Caprese and Chiusi, and of Francesca di Neri di Miniato del Sera.

1481. Death of Michelangelo's mother.

1488, APRIL 1. He is accepted as an apprentice, for three years, in the workshop of Domenico and Davide Ghirlandaio.

1489–APRIL 1492. He is accepted as a pupil in Bertoldo di Giovanni's school in the Medici Gardens of San Marco. Lorenzo de' Medici invites him to live in the Palace. He sculptures the *Madonna of the Stairs* and *The Battle of Centaurs*.

1492–94. Michelangelo returns to his father's home. He carves a wooden *Crucifix* for the Monastery of Santo Spirito and a *Hercules*. Both these works have been lost.

1494, autumn. Foreseeing the imminent expulsion of Piero de' Medici, he flees from Florence and, after a brief stay in Venice, takes up residence in Bologna, where he remains almost one year. Under the protection of Gianfrancesco Aldovrandi he completes three statuettes for the Tomb of San Domenico.

1495. Michelangelo returns to Florence. He executes a *Young St John* for Lorenzo di Pierfrancesco de' Medici and a *Sleeping Cupid*, which is sold in Rome as an ancient sculpture. These works have been lost.

1496, JUNE 25. He arrives in Rome and has dealings with Cardinal Riario, with Jacopo Galli—for whom he sculptures a *Bacchus* and a *Cupid-Apollo* (lost)—and with Cardinal Jean Bilhères who asks him to execute the *Pietà*, now in St Peter's.

1498, AUGUST 27. He obtains the contract for the *Pietà* (St Peter's).

1501, JUNE 5. Contract for the sculptures of the Piccolomini Altar in the Duomo at Siena.

1501, AUGUST 16. Contract from the Office of Works of Santa Maria del Fiore for a statue of *David*.

1502, AUGUST 12. Contract from the Signoria of Florence for a bronze *David*.

1503, APRIL 24. The Office of Works of Santa Maria del Fiore gives Michelangelo a commission for the statues of the twelve Apostles. In 1503 he roughs out *St Matthew*.

1504, AUGUST. Gonfaloniere Pier Soderini entrusts Michelangelo with a fresco for the Council Hall in the Palazzo Vecchio. In October he begins the preparatory drawing for the *Battle of Cascina*.

1505, MARCH. Michelangelo goes to Rome to make arrangements in connexion with the Tomb of Julius II.

1505, APRIL 17. He returns to Florence.

1505, MAY–DECEMBER. He is in Carrara supervising the excavation of marble and roughing out sculptures for the Tomb of Julius II.

1506, AUGUST 17. Incensed because the Pope refuses to see him, he returns to Florence. The following day the foundation-stone is laid for Bramante's new Basilica of St Peter.

1506, NOVEMBER 27. Michelangelo goes to Bologna, having been advised by the Signoria of Florence to make his peace with the Pope. Julius II asks him to execute a bronze monument for the façade of St Petronius.

1508, FEBRUARY 21. Unveiling of the *Statue of Julius II*, above the main door of St Petronius.

1508, MAY. He begins to paint the frescoes on the ceiling of the Sistine Chapel in Rome.

1508, DECEMBER. The bronze *David*, finished by Benedetto da Rovezzano, is sent from Leghorn to Monseigneur Robertet in France.

1510, SEPTEMBER. Completion of the first half of the Sistine Chapel ceiling. Michelangelo, after a serious illness, pays brief visits to Bologna and Florence.

1511, DECEMBER 30. The leaders of a revolt against the Pope in Bolagna order the destruction of the *Statue of Julius II*.

1512, OCTOBER. Completion of the frescoes in the Sistine Chapel.

1513, MAY 6. New contract for the Tomb of Julius II.

1514, JUNE 15. Bernardo Cencio and Metello Vari order a *Risen Christ* for the Church della Minerva in Rome.

1516, JULY 8. New contract for the Tomb of Julius II.

1516, JULY 15. He is back in Carrara extracting marble for the Tomb. These journeys take place repeatedly in the course of the year.

1516, DECEMBER. Michelangelo executes drawings and a model for the façade of the Church of San Lorenzo in Florence.

1517. He journeys frequently to Carrara, Pietrasanta, and Florence to secure marbles for the Tomb and for the façade of San Lorenzo.

1517, DECEMBER. He makes more models for the façade of San Lorenzo.

1518, JANUARY 19. Contract for the façade.

1518. He is in Carrara and Pietrasanta to obtain marbles.

1519, OCTOBER 20. He suggests to the Pope a sepulchral monument to Dante in Florence.

1520, MARCH 12. Leo X releases Michelangelo from his contract for the San Lorenzo façade.

1520, NOVEMBER 23. Michelangelo submits to Cardinal Giuliano de' Medici a drawing for the Medici Tombs in the Church of San Lorenzo.

1521, MARCH. By order of Leo X the Medici Tombs are begun.

1523. The Senate of Genoa offers him three hundred ducats for a statue of Andrea Doria.

1524, autumn. Work is begun on the Biblioteca Laurenziana (Medici Library).

1525, NOVEMBER. In a letter to Fattucci, Michelangelo mentions a project for a large statue to be set up in Piazza San Lorenzo, Florence.

1529, JANUARY 1. He is elected a Magistrate of the Florentine Militia.

1529, APRIL 6. He is appointed Engineer-in-Chief of the Florence fortifications.

1529, JULY–AUGUST. He inspects the fortifications of Ferrara.

1529, SEPTEMBER 21. Fleeing Florence, he goes to Ferrara and Venice. On September 30 he is declared a rebel by the City of Florence. At the end of November he obtains a safe-conduct to re-enter Florence where he is once again concerned with fortifications.

1530. He resumes work at the Medici Tombs.

1531, NOVEMBER 21. New arrangements for the Tomb of Julius II.

1532, APRIL 29. New contract for the Tomb of Julius II.

1534, SEPTEMBER 25. Death of Michelangelo's father.

1535, SEPTEMBER 1. He is appointed by Paul III Painter, Sculptor, and Architect of the Vatican Palace.

1536. He meets Vittoria Colonna.

1536, spring. He begins to paint the fresco of the *Last Judgment*.

1537, DECEMBER 10. He is made a Roman citizen.

1539. He presents Donato Giannotti with a bust of *Brutus*.

1541, OCTOBER 31. First showing of the *Last Judgment*.

1541, DECEMBER 25. Official unveiling of the *Last Judgment*.

1542, AUGUST 20. Final contract for the Tomb of Julius II.

1542, autumn. Michelangelo begins to work on the frescoes in the Pauline Chapel.

1545. Completion of the Tomb of Julius II in the Church of San Pietro in Vincoli in Rome.

1546. He presents Roberto Strozzi with the two *Slaves* intended originally for the Tomb of Julius II.

45

1546, OCTOBER 3. Death of Antonio da Sangallo. Michelangelo succeeds him as Director of Works for the Farnese Palace and Chief of the Borgo fortifications.

1546–47. During these years, presumably, Michelangelo designed the new Piazza and buildings of Rome's Capitoline Hill.

1547, FEBRUARY 25. Death of Vittoria Colonna.

1549–50. He completes the two great frescoes upon the side walls of the Pauline Chapel: one portraying the Crucifixion of St Peter and the other the Conversion of St Paul.

1549. Benedetto Varchi publishes his *Two Lessons* in which he illustrates a sonnet by Michelangelo.

1553. Michelangelo works on the *Pietà* for the Duomo at Florence. Ascanio Condivi publishes his *Life of Michelangelo*.

1555, MARCH 23. Death of Julius III; on April 9, Marcellus II is elected Pope. He favors Michelangelo's enemies. The master is thinking of returning to Florence, but the Pope dies suddenly and on May 23 of the same year Paul IV is elected. The new Pontiff reinstates Michelangelo as Chief Architect of St Peter's and keeps him in Rome to work on the great Dome of St Peter's.

1557–58. Work is begun on a wooden model of the Dome.

1560–61. He designs the Church of Santa Maria degli Angeli in the ancient Baths of Diocletian and a bronze altar canopy for the same church. The canopy was later executed by Jacopo del Duca.

1563, DECEMBER 28. He writes to his nephew Lionardo that he has been unable to answer his letters because his hand "serves him no longer," adding that in future he will get others to write his letters and he will sign them.

1564, FEBRUARY 18, Friday. In the evening, as the church bells announce the *Ave Maria*, Michelangelo dies in Rome, in the house of Macel de' Corvi.

MICHELANGELO'S SCULPTURE

Plate 1

MADONNA OF THE STAIRS. *Shallow relief in marble, 55.5 × 40.** Florence, Casa Buonarroti*. Datable about 1490–92, when Michelangelo was a guest of Lorenzo il Magnifico. This work, influenced by Donatello, is Michelangelo's earliest existing sculpture. It is mentioned by Vasari in his *Lives*.

Plate 2

THE BATTLE OF CENTAURS. *Half-relief in marble, unfinished, 90.5 × 90.5. Florence, Casa Buonarroti*. Probably executed shortly after the *Madonna of the Stairs*. Condivi and Vasari state that the subject may have been suggested by Poliziano, but while Condivi describes it as the *Rape of Dejanira and the Battle of Centaurs*, Vasari calls it the *Battle between Hercules and the Centaurs*. Tolnay believes it represents the Rape of Deidameia as narrated by Ovid (*Metamorphosis*, XII, 1, 210). Critics have found in this work stylistic and iconographic derivations from ancient Roman sarcophagi, from Giovanni Pisano, Donatello, and from a relief of a battle by Bertoldo di Giovanni, now in the Museo Nazionale at Florence. (See also plates 3–5.)

Plate 3

THE BATTLE OF CENTAURS. Detail.

Plate 4

THE BATTLE OF CENTAURS. Detail: view from the left.

Plate 5

THE BATTLE OF CENTAURS. Detail: view from the right.

Plate 6

ST PROCULUS. *Marble statuette, 58.5 (with base). Bologna, Basilica of San Domenico, Tomb of St Dominic*. During his stay in Bologna in 1494–95, Michelangelo was entrusted by Gian-francesco Aldovrandi with ornamenting the Tomb of St Dominic. (For the history of this masterpiece of Italian sculpture see the principal works of Cesare Gnudi: *Niccolò dell'Arca* and *Nicola, Arnolfo, Lapo*.) During that period Michelangelo carved the two statuettes of *St Proculus* and *St Petronius* and an *Angel Holding a Candlestick* (see plates 7–10). Originally the statue of *St Proculus* held a spear in its hand. It fell before 1572 and was restored during the same century. Neither Condivi nor Vasari mention this work, attributed to Michelangelo by Leonardo Alberti in 1535. Tolnay sees in it traces of Donatello's *St George* and Longhi finds some influence of Ercole de' Roberti.

Plate 7

ST PETRONIUS. *Marble statuette, height 64 (with base). Bologna, Basilica of San Domenico, Tomb of St Dominic*. (See comment on plate 6.) The statue's head was removed and later replaced. Both Condivi and Vasari mention this work, obviously imitative of the style of Jacopo della

* All dimensions are given in centimeters.

Quercia, though Longhi has also pointed out some connexions with Tura's art. Gnudi, who claims that the statue was begun by Niccolò dell'Arca, has noted some touches that were typical of dell'Arca.

Plate 8
ANGEL HOLDING A CANDLESTICK *Marble statuette, height 51.5 (with base). Bologna, Basilica of San Domenico, Tomb of St Dominic.* (See comment on plate 6.) This is the counterpart of a similar angel on the left, by Niccolò dell'Arca, which was believed by some critics of the last century to be by Michelangelo. Noted by Condivi and Vasari. (See also plates 9–10.)

Plate 9
ANGEL HOLDING A CANDLESTICK Front view.

Plate 10
ANGEL HOLDING A CANDLESTICK Detail: the head.

Plate 11
BACCHUS. *Marble statue, height 203 (with base). Florence, Museo Nazionale (Bargello).* Michelangelo received the commission for this work from the Roman banker, Jacopo Galli, and he executed it in Rome in 1496–97. We learn from Condivi that the statue's right hand was broken off at the beginning of the sixteenth century but replaced before 1550. Acquired by Francesco de' Medici in 1572, it was transferred to Florence the following century. During the nineteenth century it was moved from the Galleria del Granduca to the Bargello. (See also plates 12–13.)

Plate 12
BACCHUS. Detail: torso, rear view.

Plate 13
BACCHUS. Detail: the head.

Plate 14
PIETÀ. (*Also known as the* Madonna della Febbre.) *Marble group, height 174, width of base 195. Rome, Basilica of St Peter, Vatican City.* Commissioned by Cardinal Jean Bilhères de Lagraulas, of France,* before November 18, 1497. The contract is dated August 27, 1498. This group, completed in 1499, is Michelangelo's only signed work: on a band across the Virgin's tunic is written: MICHAEL–ANGELUS –BONAROTUS–FLORENT (INUS)–FACIE-BAT. The sculpture was originally placed in the Chapel of the King of France in St Peter's and moved several times until, in 1749, it was taken to the first chapel on the north side of the Basilica, where it can be seen today. Longhi thinks that earlier sculptures of the same subject by Ercole de' Roberti may have set precedents for this *Pietà*. Iconographical derivations from Nordic art have also been noted. (See also plates 15–17 and color plate I.)

Plate 15
PIETÀ. Detail: the Virgin's profile.

Plate 16
PIETÀ. Detail; head of Christ.

Color Plate I
PIETÀ. Detail of plate 14.

Plate 17
PIETÀ. Detail: the Virgin's head.

* Some scholars (Tolnay, Vasari, Goldscheider) state that Cardinal Jean de Villiers de la Groslaye commissioned the work.

Plate 18

MADONNA AND CHILD. *Marble group, height 128 (with base). Bruges, Church of Notre-Dame.* Thode dates it from 1497. Tolnay believes it was done in the spring and summer of 1501, before the marble statue of *David.* Michelangelo sold this group in 1506 to the heirs of Giovanni and Alessandro Moscheroni (or Mouscron), who took it to Bruges. Information about the iconography of this work is given in Tolnay's books (see Bibliographical Note) and in Toesca's contribution on this subject in *Enciclopedia Italiana.* View from the left. (See also plates 19–21.)

Plate 19

MADONNA AND CHILD. Front view.

Plate 20

MADONNA AND CHILD. Detail: head of the Virgin.

Plate 21

MADONNA AND CHILD. Detail: head of the Child.

Plate 22

ST PAUL. *Marble statuette, height about 120. Siena, Duomo, Piccolomini Altar.* This altar was constructed between 1481 and 1485, by Andrea Bregno for Cardinal Francesco Todeschini-Piccolomini. After Pietro Torrigiani had done a statuette of St Francis, the Cardinal entrusted Michelangelo with the execution of fifteen statuettes of Saints and Apostles to serve as decorations for the altar. The contract was signed on June 5, 1501. Michelangelo only executed four statues: this one and the three (plates 23–25) which he delivered in 1504. Letters by Michelangelo and his father, Ludovico, inform us that the statuettes were actually executed

from Michelangelo's designs by Baccio da Montelupo. Distinct qualities would suggest, however, that Michelangelo himself did some work on the statues of *SS Paul and Peter.*

Plate 23

ST PETER. *Marble statuette, height about 120. Siena, Duomo, Piccolomini Altar.* (See comment on plate 22.) Longhi believes that an idea for this work can be seen in a drawing by the artist in the British Museum.

Plate 24

ST PIUS. *Marble statuette, height about 120. Siena, Duomo, Piccolomini Altar.* (See comment on plate 22.)

Plate 25

ST GREGORY. *Marble statuette, height about 120. Siena, Duomo, Piccolomini Altar.* (See comment on plate 22.)

Plate 26

DAVID. *Marble statue, height 434 (with base). Florence, Galleria dell' Accademia di Belle Arti.* In August 1501 the Office of Works of the Duomo in Florence commissioned Michelangelo to do a figure of David from a large block of marble out of which, in 1464, Agostino di Duccio had unsuccessfully tried to carve a statue for one of the Duomo's spires. By April 1504, Michelangelo finished the statue, and a committee of Florence's most eminent artists decided to place it in front of the Signoria Palace. The figure's left arm, broken in 1527, was restored under Cosimo I. In 1873, the statue was moved to the Accademia and a copy replaced it in the square. Tolnay writes that Michelangelo was inspired by the recurrent figure of Hercules on ancient sarcophagi. (See also plates 27–29.)

49

Plate 27

DAVID. Detail: torso, rear view.

Plate 28

DAVID. Detail: profile.

Plate 29

DAVID. Detail: head, front view.

Plate 30

THE PITTI MADONNA. *Circular relief, marble, vertical diameter 85.5, horizontal diameter 82. Florence, Museo Nazionale (Bargello).* Vasari reports that this work was executed for Bartolommeo Pitti, from whose family it passed to the Guicciardini. It was purchased for the Florence Gallery in 1823 and was transferred to the Bargello in 1873. The date of execution is a matter of some controversy, but it can safely be fixed between 1504 and 1505. (See also plates 31–32.)

Plate 31

THE PITTI MADONNA. Detail: head of the Virgin.

Plate 32

THE PITTI MADONNA. Detail: head of the Child.

Color Plate II

LORENZO DE' MEDICI. Detail of plate 50.

Plate 33

THE TADDEI MADONNA. *Circular relief, marble, unfinished, diameter 109. London, Royal Academy.* This work was executed almost at the same time as *The Pitti Madonna.* Wölfflin and Tolnay date it about 1505–06. Varchi and Vasari claim that it was commissioned by Taddeo Taddei. Purchased in Rome in 1823 by Sir George Beaumont, who presented it to the Royal Academy. Tolnay believes that some details were retouched by an assistant.

Plate 34

ST MATTHEW. *Marble sculpture, unfinished, height 261. Florence, Galleria dell'Accademia di Belle Arti.* In April 1503 the directors of the Wool Guild commissioned twelve statues of the Apostles for the Church of Santa Maria del Fiore. This was the only statue which Michelangelo roughed out. Since the contract was nullified in December 1505, the execution must have taken place prior to that date, but Tolnay, Ollendorfer, and Bertini believe this figure to be the one that Michelangelo was working on in the summer of 1506. This is apparently confirmed by a letter written by Soderini in November of that year. This is the first great example of the master's suggestive "incompleteness," evident somewhat in his previous reliefs. The statue was moved from the Duomo to the Accademia in 1834. (See also the comment on plate 35.)

Plate 35

ST MATTHEW. Detail: the head.

Plate 36

THE DYING SLAVE. *Marble sculpture, unfinished, height 229. Paris, Louvre.* This work was intended for the second version (1513) of the *Tomb of Julius II* (see plans on pp. 58–59). In 1544, Michelangelo gave this sculpture and its twin, *The Rebellious Slave,* to Roberto Strozzi, exiled in Lyons, and Strozzi, in turn, presented them to Francis I. They later became the property of the Montmorency family and then the Richelieu. They were confiscated in 1793 but redeemed in 1794 by Alexandre Lenoir. They finally went to the Louvre.

50

Many scholars have tried to explain the allegory of these two figures and also of the four *Captives* in the Florence Academy (plates 100–107). They have been variously interpreted as the Liberal Arts; the Prisoners of Death (after the disappearance of Julius II); the provinces captured by the Papal armies; the heathen nations conquered by the True Faith, and so on. (See also plate 38.)

Plate 37

THE REBELLIOUS SLAVE. *Marble sculpture, unfinished, height 215. Paris, Louvre.* A letter of 1513 proves that Michelangelo was working on this statue in that year. Like the previous figure, this one was also intended for the Tomb of Julius II. A drawing for this work is at Oxford. (See also plate 39.)

Plate 38

THE DYING SLAVE. Detail: head and shoulders.

Plate 39

THE REBELLIOUS SLAVE. Detail: head and shoulders.

Plate 40

MOSES. *Marble sculpture, height 235. Rome, Church of San Pietro in Vincoli.* Executed for the second version of the Tomb of Julius II (see plans on pp. 58–59) and ultimately located there when the monument was completed (see plate 110). Documents inform us that Michelangelo was working on this sculpture in 1515 and that he had not yet finished it in 1516. There are certain analogies between the *Moses* and the *Prophet Joel* on the ceiling of the Sistine Chapel and with the later statue of *Giuliano de' Medici* (see plate 65). (See also plates 41–43.)

Plate 41

MOSES. From the right.

Plate 42

MOSES. Detail: head, from the left.

Plate 43

MOSES. Detail: head, from the right.

Plate 44

HERCULES AND CACUS. *Fragmentary clay model, also known as* Samson and a Philistine, *height 41. Florence, Casa Buonarroti.* In 1508 the Florentine Republic planned to erect in front of the Signoria Palace, as a companion to the *David*, a *Hercules and Antaeus* by Michelangelo. This plan was not carried out. In 1525, Clement VII entrusted this task to Bandinelli, though the Signoria still favored Michelangelo. In 1528, when the Medici left the city, the City Fathers took the marble from Bandinelli and gave it to Michelangelo, who presumably then made this model. After the fall of the Republic, however, the Pope had the marble returned to Bandinelli, who executed the group still standing in front of the Palace. Springer and Wilde, however, surmise that this model may have been of a Victory intended for the Tomb of Julius II (see plan on p. 58).

Plate 45

THE RISEN CHRIST. *Marble statue, height 205. Rome, Church of Santa Maria sopra Minerva.* A first version of this statue, commissioned in 1514 by Bernardo Cencio, Maria Scapucci, and Metello Vari, which Michelangelo did not finish because the marble was defective, has been lost. From 1519 to 1520 Michelangelo worked on this second version, which he sent to Rome in 1521. Ruined by the retouching of his apprentice, Urbano, the sculpture was altered by Federico Frizzi and later by Michelangelo himself, who was not satisfied with it and would have tried a third version. Vari would not, however, consent and the statue was unveiled on December 27, 1521.

THE NEW SACRISTY OF SAN LORENZO AND THE MEDICI TOMBS

(Plates 46–89 and Color Plate II)

Because of a shortage of funds in the Papal Treasury, work on the façade of San Lorenzo in Florence had to be interrupted. Cardinal Giulio de' Medici and Pope Leo X then suggested to Michelangelo that he complete a chapel in that church, for the tombs of four Medici: Lorenzo the Magnificent and his brother Giuliano, Lorenzo Duke of Urbino, and Giuliano Duke of Nemours. Michelangelo was unwilling at first, but later accepted the commission. In January 1521 his final project had been approved, and the excavation of the marble began at Carrara.

From letters and drawings in the British Museum and in the Casa Buonarroti at Florence, we learn that initially the master had thought of grouping the four tombs in a tabernacle in the center of the Chapel. In a later project, also discarded, he placed them against the walls, in groups of two.

Work in the Chapel proceeded very slowly, for the extraction of the proper marbles was difficult and the political situation, which led to the expulsion of the Medici, tense and unstable. But in 1525 the Chapel itself was finished and work on the tombs had been proceeding for one year. Since 1521, however, there were only two tombs to be done, because those of Lorenzo the Magnificent and his brother Giuliano had been decided against. Many projected works were never executed: sculptures destined for the niches on either side of the Dukes, the *River Divinities* intended for the lower part of the sarcophagi, and of which only a mutilated model remains in the Florence Academy (see plates 90–91), stuccoes and frescoes for the walls and dome.

Besides some friezes and other decorations (plates 82–84), Michelangelo's work includes the two great groups of *Lorenzo de' Medici, Duke of Urbino* above *Dusk* and *Dawn* (plates 46, 48 and 50–64), and of *Giuliano de' Medici, Duke of Nemours* above *Night* and *Day* (plates 47, 49, and 65–81); the statue of the *Madonna and Child* (plates 86–89), over the altar by the entrance to the Chapel (plate 85), flanked by the statues of *SS Cosmo and Damian*, which are the work of Montorsoli and Raffaello da Montelupo under Michelangelo's direction.

In 1533 the finishing touches to the sculptures were still under way.

In 1524 and 1525 Michelangelo had also planned the tombs of the Medici Popes, Leo X and Clement VII, which were to have been erected, according to his first project, in a small sacristy next door to the Sagrestia Vecchia of San Lorenzo. He later decided to place them against the walls of the church's choir. These plans, of which some drawings have remained, were never carried out.

Plate 46

TOMB OF LORENZO DE' MEDICI, DUKE OF URBINO. (See also plate 48.)

Plate 47

TOMB OF GIULIANO DE' MEDICI, DUKE OF NEMOURS. (See also plate 49.)

Plate 48

TOMB OF LORENZO DE' MEDICI. Side view.

Plate 49

TOMB OF GIULIANO DE' MEDICI. Side view.

Plate 50

LORENZO DE' MEDICI. *Marble sculpture, height 178.* Some minor points were done by Montorsoli. Begun in 1524, it was still unfinished in 1531. It has been known since the sixteenth century as the "Pensieroso" (the Thinker). (See also plates 51–53 and color plate II.)

Plate 51

LORENZO DE' MEDICI. Detail: the bust.

Plate 52

LORENZO DE' MEDICI. Detail: the arm and the hand.

Color Plate II

LORENZO DE' MEDICI. Detail of plate 50.

Plate 53

LORENZO DE' MEDICI. Detail: the head.

Plate 54

DUSK. *Marble sculpture, unfinished, length 195.* Executed between 1524 and 1531. Tolnay believes that in conceiving this figure Michelangelo was inspired by the sculptures of mountain and river divinities on the Arch of Septimius Severus in Rome. (See also plates 56, 58, 60, 64.)

Plate 55

DAWN. *Marble sculpture, length 203.* Executed between 1524 and 1531. The Arch of Septimius Severus again, submits Tolnay, is the source of inspiration. (See also plates 57, 59, 61–63.)

Plate 56

DUSK. From the rear.

Plate 57

DAWN. From the rear.

Plate 58

DUSK. From the side.

Plate 59

DAWN. From the side.

Plate 60

DUSK. Detail: bust.

Plate 61

DAWN. Detail: bust.

Plate 62

DAWN. Detail: bust.

Plate 63

DAWN: Detail: head.

Plate 64

DUSK. Detail: head.

Plate 65

GIULIANO DE' MEDICI. *Marble sculpture, height 173.* Some collaboration by Montorsoli. Begun in 1526, it was still unfinished in July 1533. Its analogies with the *Moses* and with the figure of the *Prophet Joel* in the Sistine Chapel have already been mentioned (see plate 40).

Plate 66

GIULIANO DE' MEDICI. From the rear.

Plate 67

GIULIANO DE' MEDICI. Detail: the head.

Plate 68

GIULIANO DE' MEDICI. Detail: armor, from the rear.

Plate 69

GIULIANO DE' MEDICI. Detail: the hand.

Plate 70

NIGHT. *Marble sculpture, length 194.* Executed between 1526 and 1531. The figure's pose is copied after an ancient Leda carved upon a sarcophagus, and Michelangelo used it again for his drawing of *Leda*. (See also plates 72, 74, 76–79.)

Plate 71

DAY. *Marble sculpture, unfinished, length 185.* Executed between 1526 and 1533. (See also plates 73, 75, 80–81.)

Plate 72

NIGHT. From the rear.

Plate 73

DAY. From the rear.

Plate 74

NIGHT. From the side.

Plate 75

DAY. From the side.

Plate 76

NIGHT. Detail: the head.

Plate 77

NIGHT. Detail: the head.

Plate 78

NIGHT. Detail: the allegorical owl.

Plate 79

NIGHT. Detail: the mask.

Plate 80

DAY. Detail: bust, from the rear.

Plate 81

DAY. Detail: the head.

Plate 82

FRIEZES IN THE MEDICI CHAPEL. *Friezes of masks on the left of the statue of* Night.

Plate 83

FRIEZES IN THE MEDICI CHAPEL. *Capitals of the pillars above the tombs.*

Plate 84

FRIEZES IN THE MEDICI CHAPEL. *Vases on the side tabernacles.* The first one on the left bears the Medici arms.

Plate 85

MEDICI CHAPEL. The wall by the entrance, with the altar on which the *Madonna and Child* are flanked by *SS Cosmo and Damian*, by Montorsoli and Raffaello da Montelupo. (See plates 86–89.)

Plate 86

MADONNA AND CHILD. *Marble sculpture, unfinished, height 226.* This statue was mentioned in 1521, but it was still unfinished in September 1531. Tolnay believes it to be a second version, recarved from the same block as the first one. Two pen-and-ink drawings of the Madonna have remained. (See also plates 87–89.)

Plate 87

MADONNA AND CHILD. From the front.

Plate 88

MADONNA AND CHILD. Detail: upper part.

Plate 89

MADONNA AND CHILD. Detail: head of the Madonna.

Plate 90

MODEL FOR A RIVER GOD. *Sculpture in wood, wool, and clay, length 180. Florence, Galleria dell'Accademia di Belle Arti*. Records of 1524 mention two large models for river divinities which were later placed under the statues of *Dusk* and *Day* in the Medici Chapel; it is also known that in 1526 their execution in marble had not yet begun. This sculpture, therefore, could be dated about 1524. The model was presented by Cosimo I to Bartolommeo Ammannati, who donated it to the Florence Academy in 1583. (See also plate 91.)

Plate 91

MODEL FOR A RIVER GOD. Another view.

Plate 92

THE CROUCHING BOY. *Marble sculpture, unfinished, height 54. Leningrad, Hermitage*. Datable about 1524. This statuette is included in a drawing for the Tomb of Lorenzo de' Medici, where it can be seen upon the upper frame, but this project was not carried out by Michelangelo. Some critics believe that the work is by a pupil from a drawing by Michelangelo (Kriegbaum thinks that the pupil may have been Tribolo, while for Wittkower he could have been Pierino da Vinci). The sculpture was sent from the

Medici Collection to the Hermitage during the eighteenth century. (See also plate 93.)

Plate 93

THE CROUCHING BOY. From the side.

Plate 94

DAVID-APOLLO. *Marble sculpture, unfinished, height 146. Florence, Museo Nazionale (Bargello)*. Recorded by Vasari as *Apollo*, and as *David* in the inventory of the Grand Duke Cosimo's Collection (1533). Michelangelo is known to have worked at this statue in 1531 and some critics (Popp and Tolnay) believe that he began it in 1525–26. Some think that it was intended for the Medici Chapel in San Lorenzo. While the majority of critics generally favor the *David* designation, Tolnay suggests that when Baccio Valori asked Michelangelo for one of his works, the master changed a *David* he was roughing out into an *Apollo*. From the Medici Collection the statue went to the Boboli Gardens, then to the Uffizi, and finally to the Bargello. (See also plate 95.)

Plate 95

DAVID-APOLLO. From the side.

Plate 96

THE VICTORY. *Marble sculpture, height 261. Florence, Signoria Palace*. The figure of the vanquished barbarian is roughed out. Neither the date of the execution nor the purpose of the statue are definitely known. Critics are still arguing the question. It was probably executed between 1532 and 1534 (Kriegbaum dates it as early as 1506), and intended perhaps for the Tomb of Julius II (see plan on p. 58), but Toesca, Alazard, and others have doubts about this theory. Wittkower thinks, mistakenly, that the head of the victorious youth is Vincenzo Danti's. Lionardo Buonarroti and Daniele da Volterra wanted this statue to decorate Michelangelo's tomb. (See also plates 97–99.)

Color Plate III
BRUTUS. Detail of plate 108.

Plate 97
THE VICTORY. From the side.

Plate 98
THE VICTORY. Detail: the victor's head.

Plate 99
THE VICTORY. Detail: the barbarian's head.

Plate 100
YOUTHFUL CAPTIVE. *Marble sculpture, unfinished, height 235. Florence, Galleria dell'Accademia di Belle Arti.* The date of this and of the other three figures of *Slaves* or *Captives* is controversial. They were certainly intended for the Tomb of Julius II (see plans on pp. 58–59); Justi, Thode, Kriegbaum, and Laux set the date of their execution at 1519; Toesca and Carli prefer 1520–22; Popp favors 1527–30 and Tolnay submits a period between September 1534 and April 1536, believing that the figures were destined for the fifth version of the Tomb. The four *Captives* and *The Victory* were presented, after Michelangelo's death, by his nephew Lionardo to the Grand Duke Cosimo I, who asked Buontalenti to use the *Captives* as part of the grotto in the Boboli Gardens, from where they were moved to the Academy in 1908. (See plate 101 and comment on plate 36.)

Plate 101
YOUTHFUL CAPTIVE. From the side.

Plate 102
BEARDED CAPTIVE. *Marble sculpture, unfinished, height 248. Florence, Galleria dell'Accademia di Belle Arti.* See comment on plate 100. Popp surmises that a small terracotta in the British Museum was the model for this statue. (See also plate 103.)

Plate 103
BEARDED CAPTIVE. From the side.

Plate 104
ATLAS. *Marble sculpture, unfinished, height 208. Florence, Galleria dell'Accademia di Belle Arti.* From the front. (See comment on plate 100 and see also plate 105.)

Plate 105
ATLAS. From the side.

Plate 106
AWAKENING CAPTIVE. *Marble sculpture, unfinished, height 267. Florence, Galleria dell'Accademia di Belle Arti.* From the front. (See comment on plate 100 and see also plate 107.)

Plate 107
AWAKENING CAPTIVE. From the side.

Plate 108
BRUTUS. *Marble bust, unfinished, height 95. Florence, Museo Nazionale (Bargello).* According to Vasari, this bust was executed in Rome, after 1539, for Cardinal Niccolò Ridolfi, following a suggestion by Donato Giannotti. Michelangelo's apprentice, Tiberio Calcagni, finished some of the minor parts. An inscription on a bronze plate on the base reads:

M.A.F.B. // DUM · BRUTI · EFFI-
GIEM // SCULPTOR · DE · MARMORE
· DUCIT // IN · MENTEM · SCELERIS
· VENIT // ET · ABSTINUIT (Michelangelo Buonarroti made this work.
While the sculptor was carving the
likeness of Brutus out of the marble,
he recalled the latter's crime, and so
carved no more.) This inscription is
attributed to Bembo by Richardson,
and provides an interesting ethical
explanation for Michelangelo's unfinished sculptures. The bust was
inspired by busts of ancient Roman
emperors, particularly those of Cara-
calla. Vasari says that it was actually
copied from an old engraving that
belonged to Giuliano Cesarino.
Protheim claims that the bust is an
idealized portrait of Lorenzino de'
Medici. The sculpture was acquired
by the Grand Duke Francesco de'
Medici during the last decade of the
sixteenth century. (See also plate 109)

Plate 109
BRUTUS. Detail: the head.

Plate 110
TOMB OF JULIUS II. *Rome, Basilica
of San Pietro in Vincoli*. Final version,
that is to say, the sixth plan, in
chronological order, drawn up by
Michelangelo, who from 1505 to
1545 was tormented by what he
described as "this tragedy of the
Sepulchre." Given here are the main
facts about this long, controversial
affair and the Tomb's various projects.
On pp. 58–59 are four attempts at
reconstructing the plans. These re-
constructions are based upon those
suggested by Tolnay from the illus-
tration by Denise Fossard.
   In 1505, Pope Julius II called
Michelangelo to Rome and entrusted
him with his own sepulchral monument, which was to be—said Julius
—"the grandest ever built." The

mausoleum was to be placed in the
apse of the new Basilica of St Peter.
Michelangelo produced a plan which
the Pope approved, and then proceeded to Carrara to choose the
marbles and arrange for their excavation. He stayed there eight months.
On returning to Rome he found that
the Pope had changed his mind and
appointed Bramante Architect of St
Peter's. Disgusted by the scheming
of his rivals, Michelangelo left Rome
on August 17, 1506.
   Since the drawings are lost, any
reconstruction of this first version of
the Tomb must remain purely con-
jectural, based as it is on reports by
Vasari and Condivi, who partly con-
tradicted one another. Generally
speaking, though, this much may be
said about it: the Tomb was to
consist of a rectangular tabernacle,
of approximately 20 × 30 feet, free-
standing, that is, not set up against
a wall. In the lower part, defined by
protruding plinths supporting figures
of *Slaves*, there would be niches with
statues of *Victories* between pillars;
one or two doors were to lead into
the funerary chamber containing the
sarcophagus. In the upper part,
above a ledge, were to have been four
seated figures, including the *Moses*;
behind them the top of the tabernacle
would rise, in the shape of a shortened
pyramid, decorated with bronze reliefs and other sculptures. At the very
top were to have been two allegories,
Heaven and *Earth*, supporting a catafalque with the figure of the Pope.
Tolnay has published a drawing from
the Ambrosiana Gallery in Milan,
representing a plan for a catafalque
for Michelangelo. An inscription
states that it is derived from the first
version of the Tomb of Julius II; it
offers, certainly, valid elements for
the reconstruction of the original
design.

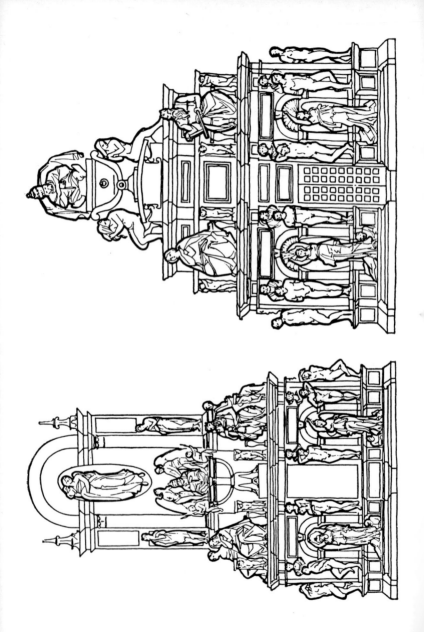

First, second, third, and fifth versions of the *Tomb of Julius II* as reconstructed by Charles de Tolnay.

Julius II died in February 1513. In May of that year Michelangelo signed a new contract with the Pope's heirs for a different monument.

The sources at our disposal for reconstructing this second version are the contract itself and several drawings, of which there is one in Berlin and one in the Uffizi, Florence. The latter is a copy, attributed to Aristotile da Sangallo, from the original model by Michelangelo.

An essential change from the first version is that the Tomb—which was no longer to be built in St Peter's —would now be erected against a wall and would have no funerary chamber. This project, furthermore, was on a much larger scale. While the lower part was to remain more or less the same as for the first version, with the *Slaves* upon plinths and the *Victories* in niches, a platform above the ledge was to support a bier with the Pope's statue on top, held up or surrounded by four figures. For the main circle of figures, instead of the four envisaged in the first project, there were to be six seated statues. Behind the bier an enormous niche some twenty-four feet high was to contain a *Madonna and Child* enclosed in an almond-shaped frame. The niche was to be surrounded by five great statues and other architectural elements. With this plan in mind, Michelangelo sculptured the two *Captives*, now in the Louvre, and began working on the *Moses*.

In July 1516 a third contract was signed which brought further alterations to the plan. Some sketches of this third version are now in the Casa Buonarroti. The mausoleum was much reduced in depth, becoming at most a façade with narrow sides, and in each side niche there was to be a statue, flanked with pillars, against which the *Slaves* were to stand. The front of the lower part was similar to the one projected in 1513 and in the central rectangle of that side a bronze relief was to be placed. The upper level, however, was changed: it became as wide as the lower one and divided in compartments along the lines of the lower pillars; finally the structure was to be crowned by a cornice, surmounted by a low, flat roof. The niche with the *Madonna and Child* remained, but immediately beneath it a group was to appear, representing the dead Pontiff held up by two figures; other smaller niches were to enclose four great seated figures. The whole monument was to be decorated with reliefs in marble and bronze.

In 1522 the Rovere family, heirs of Julius, wanted Michelangelo to return them the money they had advanced for the Tomb, and in 1524 they threatened to take legal action. The sculptor then quickly devised a new, simplified version of the monument, requiring less time for execution. He sent his new plan to Rome on October 16, 1526, but the Roveres would not accept it. This fourth version has been lost, but Tolnay, from sketches drawn in those years and which seem to be connected with that work, submits the theory that Michelangelo had compromised by reducing the Tomb to a simple façade with many niches, with the Pope's seated figure in the central niche.

On November 21, 1531, the heirs were still insisting that the work be completed and that all the marbles and sculptures executed to date be employed in the finished monument.

On April 29, 1532, Michelangelo signed another contract, cancelling all previous agreements, and committing him to finish the Tomb within three years. Of this fifth version we know only that it was to be erected in San Pietro in Vincoli and that all the sculpture previously finished were to be placed in the final structure. Six great figures were to be included in it, carved personally by Michelangelo. A number of drawings provide some detailed information, and in general one may assume that this Tomb was fairly similar to the one projected in 1516. It is possible that Michelangelo executed *The Victory* in the Signoria Palace and the four *Captives* in the Galleria della Accademia for this version of the monument, though some critics believe those works to have been intended for other uses, and indeed done in some other period of the sculptor's life.

On August 20, 1542, the last contract was signed. The three years stipulated for the completion had elapsed long before, while Michelangelo was painting his Vatican frescoes for Paul III. The contract for the sixth version was carried out in 1545. The Tomb now stands in San Pietro in Vincoli at Rome.

Many pupils and apprentices worked on the mausoleum, either under Michelangelo's direct supervision or from his drawings. He worked on only the statues of *Active Life* (*Leah*) and *Contemplative Life* (*Rachel*). Of all the figures he had executed for the previous plans of the Tomb only *Moses* is now there. The architecture of the upper half was the work of Giovanni di Marchesi and Francesco da Urbino, from Michelangelo's design. Other sculptures are by Donato Benti and Jacopo del Duca. Domenico Fancelli and Raffaello da Montelupo worked in succession on the figures of *The Virgin*, the *Prophet* and the *Sibyl*, which Michelangelo had roughed out in 1537, and Tommaso Boscoli sculptured the *Pope*. The ornamental elements are partly those executed for the previous projects. (See also plates 40 and 43 of *Moses*, and plates 111–113.)

Plate 111

RACHEL. *Marble sculpture, height 197. Rome, Basilica of San Pietro in Vincoli,* Tomb of Julius II. This statue was begun on July 20, 1542. Michelangelo actually finished it, instead of entrusting its completion to Raffaello da Montelupo. as he had intended. Vasari and Condivi both call this work *Contemplative Life.* Together with the figure of *Leah* it could have been derived from Dante (*Purgatory*, XXVII, 97).

Plate 112

LEAH. *Marble sculpture, height 209. Rome, Basilica of San Pietro in Vincoli,* Tomb of Julius II. Called *Active Life* by Vasari and Condivi. (See also plate 113.)

Color Plate IV

RONDANINI PIETÀ. Detail of plate 123.

Plate 113

LEAH. Detail: the head.

Plate 114

PIETÀ. *Marble, unfinished, height 226. Florence, Duomo.* This group, executed by Michelangelo for his funerary chapel—which was to be in Santa Maria Maggiore at Rome—was mentioned by Vasari in 1550 and Condivi reports that the master was still working on it in 1553. According to Vasari, Michelangelo broke off Christ's arm during the execution and left the work unfinished. He destroyed the arm and also Christ's left leg. In 1561 Michelangelo presented the sculpture to Francesco

61

Bandini. Later Tiberio Calcagni restored the group—except for the leg—and continued the work, especially the figure of Magdalen. The face of *Nicodemus* (plate 118) is said by Vasari to be a self-portrait. There are many copies of this group. Cosimo III had it moved to Florence, where it was placed in San Lorenzo. (See also plates 115–18.)

Plate 115

PIETÀ. From the front.

Plate 116

PIETÀ. From the rear.

Plate 117

PIETÀ. Detail: upper part.

Plate 118

PIETÀ. Detail: Nicodemus's head, said to be a self-portrait of Michelangelo.

Plate 119

PALESTRINA PIETÀ. *Marble, unfinished, height 253. Florence, Galleria dell' Accademia di Belle Arti.* Originally placed in the Chapel of the Barberini Palace at Palestrina, this sculpture was first attributed to Michelangelo by L. Cecconi in *Storia di Palestrina* (Ascoli, 1576). It is not recorded in any early documents. Toesca ("Un capolavoro di Michelangelo: La Pietà di Palestrina", in *Le Arti*, December–January 1938–39) suggested that the group could be one recorded in an old treatise on painting and sculpture written in Rome in 1652 and said to have been "found buried in a room on the ground floor (of Michelangelo's home) and which is now on public display in Rome." The Barberini family were said to have been advised by Pietro da Cortona to purchase the sculpture. After Cecconi, F. Gori (in 1875) and A. Grenier (in 1907) conjectured that Michelangelo was its sculptor. This attribution was accepted by A. Venturi, by Berenson (with reservations), and with full certainty by P. Toesca, supported by, among others, V. Mariani, A. Bertini, M. Marangoni, F. Kriegbaum, and E. Carli. But the work had been thought for a long time to be after Michelangelo, even if not an original. Tradition linked it with Giovan Lorenzo Bernini (see Nibby, *Analisi storico-tipografica dei dintorni di Roma*, 1837), though no stylistic element would confirm it. The attribution to Michelangelo is not accepted, among others, by E. Steinmann, E. Popp, H. Thode, C. de Tolnay. The latter believes the sculptor to have been one of Michelangelo's apprentices who combined motifs from many works by the master; the shape and thickness of the block (which is a piece of classic entablature) are, in Tolnay's view, different from the ones preferred by Michelangelo, and the workmanship betrays qualities which are unusual for him. This work may have been retouched at the time of its removal to Palestrina. (See also plates 120–22.)

Plate 120

PALESTRINA PIETÀ. Detail: upper part.

Plate 121

PALESTRINA PIETÀ. Detail: the Magdalen.

Plate 122

PALESTRINA PIETÀ. Detail: the body of Christ.

Plate 123

RONDANINI PIETÀ. *Marble, height 195. Milan, Civiche Raccolte d' Arte*

(*Castello Sforzesco*). This admirable work was Michelangelo's last, for he was working on it just before he died in February 1564. For many centuries it remained in the courtyard of the Rondanini Palace in Rome, before becoming the property of Count Vimercati-Sanseverino's family from whom the Commune of Milan purchased it in 1952. In or about 1555, Michelangelo is known to have made good progress with a *Pietà*. Earlier he had made one for the Duomo at Florence, but it was damaged. (Three drawings at Oxford are related to the new version.) But this, too, was abandoned. Later, he took it up again, but transformed it radically. When, as Vasari says, "the old man found it necessary to have pieces of marble so that he could spend a part of each day with his hammer and chisel." The group is therefore composed of some entirely finished parts, not reworked at all, from the first version (such as the right arm, detached from the body, and the legs of Christ), and of other parts at which he was working or which were deliberately left unfinished. (Notice, for instance, on the veil covering the Virgin's head, the roughing out of a previous face,

turned in another direction.) At a later date the base was cut in front and inscribed SS PIETÀ BY MICHELANGELO BUONAROTA. This group is mentioned in Michelangelo's Inventories of February 19 and of March 17, 1564. Tolnay claims that some elements from the original version are evident in the *Palestrina Pietà*. Tolnay also claims that a *Pietà*, by Taddeo Zuccaro, in the Borghese Gallery in Rome, is a free copy of the early version of this *Pietà*. (See also plates 124–28 and color-plate IV.)

Plate 124
RONDANINI PIETÀ. Another view.

Plate 125
RONDANINI PIETÀ. From the side.

Plate 126
RONDANINI PIETÀ. From the side.

Plate 127
RONDANINI PIETÀ. Detail: the two faces.

Plate 128
RONDANINI PIETÀ. Detail: the two faces.

LOST SCULPTURE

HEAD OF A FAUN. Mentioned by Vasari and Condivi as Michelangelo's first sculpture, done in about 1489. Some critics wrongly assumed this to be the *Mask of a Faun* in the Bargello or the *Head of a Cyclops*, also in the Bargello (A. Venturi).

CRUCIFIX. *Wood. Formerly at Florence, in the Church of Santo Spirito.* Probably carved in 1492. Thode identified it with a Crucifix in the sacristy of that church, but Tolnay dismissed it as a copy made in the last twenty years of the sixteenth century. Bertini finds no justification for even considering it a copy.

HERCULES. *Marble figure, height approximately 250. Formerly at Fontainebleau, Jardin de l'Estang.* Recorded by Condivi and Vasari. Executed before 1494. Tolnay claims that the back of this figure was reproduced in an engraving by Israel Sylvestre of the Jardin de l'Estang. Bajersdorfer, Justi, Liphart-Rathshoff, and Bertini believe that this figure inspired a *Hercules* in the amphitheater of the Boboli Gardens in Florence.

YOUNG ST JOHN. *Formerly in the possession of Lorenzo di Pierfrancesco de' Medici.* Executed after Michelangelo's return to Florence from Bologna, between 1495 and 1496. Bode mistakenly identified it with a sculpture in the Staatliches Museen at Berlin, but Tolnay believes this is late sixteenth century, in the manner of the Francavilla School. Valentiner thought it might be a statue in the Morgan Library, which Middeldorf and Ragghianti, however, attribute to Rustici and Tolnay to Silvio Costini. Gomez-Moreno attempted to identify it with another *Young St John* in the Chapel of the Savior in Ubeda.

SLEEPING CUPID. *Marble, height approximately 80. Formerly in the possession of Isabella d'Este at Mantua.* Mentioned by Condivi and Vasari. Two mistaken identifications have been made: by Symonds with a *Cupid* in the Vergilian Academy in Mantua, and by Conrad Lange with a *Cupid* in the Turin Museum.

CUPID-APOLLO. *Marble, life-size. Formerly in the Collection of Jacopo Galli, in Rome.* Recalled by Condivi and Vasari. Executed between 1496 and 1501. A. Venturi, Mac Lagan, and Jean Alazard claim this to be a sculpture in the Victoria and Albert Museum, London, but Kriegbaum, supported by Tolnay and Bertini, attributes the London statue to Vincenzo Danti, stating that it is probably a figure of Narcissus.

DAVID. *Bronze. Formerly in Bury Castle.* Commissioned in 1502 by the Maréchal Pierre de Rohan, who demanded a figure similar to Donatello's bronze *David*. The statue was

65

finished in 1508 by Benedetto da Rovezzano. Courajod thought this to be a statuette in the Louvre, where it had come from the Charles de Pulsky Collection. Pit recognized a copy of it in a model he saw in the Rijksmuseum, Amsterdam. Bajersdorfer thought he had seen a small model for this sculpture in a terracotta in the Casa Buonarroti at Florence.

JULIUS II. *Bronze. Formerly on the façade of the Church of St Petronius in Bologna.* The Pope himself had ordered Michelangelo to make it in 1506. The statue was placed there in April 1508, but the Bolognese populace destroyed it on December 30, 1511, after the return of the Bentivoglios to that city. The Pope was represented in a seated position, with his right arm raised and with the symbolic keys in his left hand.

RISEN CHRIST. *Marble statuette, unfinished.* Mentioned in the Inventory of Michelangelo's estate and in a letter by Daniele da Volterra of March 17, 1564.

DAGGER. *Formerly in the possession of Filippo Strozzi at Florence.* Mentioned in letters of 1506 and 1507.

MODEL FOR A SILVER SALT-CELLAR. Decorated with animal claws, festoons, masks, and a figure upon the lid. Made for Francesco Maria Duke of Urbino. Mentioned by Gei Staccoli in a letter of July 4, 1537.

SMALL HORSE. *Bronze.* Model for Francesco Maria Duke of Urbino, 1537.

PIETÀ. *Relief.* Executed for Vittoria Colonna, mentioned by the Bishop of Fano in a letter of 1546 to Cardinal Ercole Gonzaga. The best of many copies of this work is to be found in the Vatican Library.

SCULPTURE ATTRIBUTED TO MICHELANGELO

(Not inclusive of the attempts, previously mentioned, to locate Michelangelo's lost works.)

NUDE YOUTH. *Red terracotta. Florence, Casa Buonarroti.* Thought to have been a model for the marble *David*; Tolnay believes it to be a copy of a lost model by Michelangelo.

NUDE YOUTH. *Wax model. Florence, Casa Buonarroti.* This model too is believed by Tolnay to be a copy, perhaps, of a lost model executed in about 1505.

APOLLO AND MARSYAS. *Marble relief. New York.* Attributed to Michelangelo by Bode and Mackowsky. Tolnay sees in it Buonarroti's influence and thinks it was executed in approximately 1520.

APOLLO. *Marble statuette. Berlin, Staatliches Museen.* The attribution is by Bode. Tolnay calls it an imitation of Michelangelo's technique.

DYING ADONIS. *Marble. Florence, Museo Nazionale (Bargello).* A work by Vincenzo de' Rossi.

ST SEBASTIAN. *Marble. London, Victoria and Albert Museum.* The attribution is by Robinson. Middeldorf assigns it to Tribolo.

THE MARTYRDOM OF ST ANDREW. *Marble relief. Florence, Museo Nazionale (Bargello).* From the Board of Works of Santa Maria del Fiore in 1823, it went to the Gallery of Statues as a work done "by an unknown hand"; from 1825 it was attributed to Michelangelo. Thode ascribes it to Bandinelli, while Dami supports the traditional attribution to Michelangelo.

LOCATION OF SCULPTURE

BOLOGNA

BASILICA OF SAN DOMENICO
St Proculus (plate 6).
St Petronius (plate 7).
Angel Holding a Candlestick (plates 8–10).

BRUGES

CHURCH OF NOTRE-DAME
Madonna and Child (plates 18–21).

FLORENCE

BASILICA OF SAN LORENZO
Tomb of Lorenzo de' Medici, Duke of Urbino (plates 46, 48).
Tomb of Giuliano de' Medici, Duke of Nemours (plates 47, 49).
Lorenzo de' Medici (plates 50–53 and color plate II).
Dusk (plates 54, 56, 58, 60, 64).
Dawn (plates 55, 57, 59, 61–63).
Giuliano de' Medici (plates 65–69).
Night (plates 70, 72, 74, 76–79).
Day (plates 71, 73, 75, 80–81).
Friezes in the Medici Chapel (plates 82–84).

CASA BUONARROTI
Madonna of the Stairs (plate 1).
The Battle of Centaurs (plates 2–5).
Hercules and Cacus (plate 44).

DUOMO
Pietà (plates 114–18).

GALLERIA DELL'ACCADEMIA
DI BELLE ARTI

David (plates 26–29).
St Matthew (plates 34–35).
Model for a River God (plates 90–91).
Youthful Captive (plates 100–01).
Bearded Captive (plates 102–03).
Atlas (plate 104–05).
Awakening Captive (plates 106–07).
Palestrina Pietà (plates 119–22).

MUSEO NAZIONALE (BAR-
GELLO)
Bacchus (plates 11–13).
The Pitti Madonna (plates 30–32).
David-Apollo (plates 94–95).
Brutus (plates 108–09 and color plate III).

PALAZZO DELLA SIGNORIA
The Victory (plates 96–99).

LENINGRAD

HERMITAGE
The Crouching Boy (plates 92–93).

LONDON

ROYAL ACADEMY
The Taddei Madonna (plate 33).

MILAN

CASTELLO SFORZESCO
Rondanini Pietà (plates 123–8 and color plate IV).

PARIS

LOUVRE
The Dying Slave (plates 36, 38).
The Rebellious Slave (plates 37, 39).

ROME

St Peter's Basilica (Vatican)
Pietà (plates 14–17 and color plate I.)

Church of San Pietro in Vincoli
Moses (plates 40–43).
Tomb of Julius II (plate 110).
Rachel (plate 111).
Leah (plates 112–13).

Church of Santa Maria sopra Minerva
The Risen Christ (plate 45).

SIENA

Duomo
St Paul (plate 22).
St Peter (plate 23).
St Pius (plate 24).
St Gregory (plate 25).

SELECTED CRITICISM

To Messer Benedetto Varchi.

Messer Benedetto, so that it may be known that I have indeed received your little book, I shall reply, ignorant though I am, to some of the questions you have asked of me. I think others hold that painting is good when it moves nearer to relief, and relief is bad when it approaches painting. I used to believe, however, that sculpture was the guiding light of painting, and between the two there was the same difference as between the sun and moon. But now that I have read your book in which you say that, philosophically speaking, those things which are directed to the same purpose are really one and the same thing, I have changed my opinion: now, therefore, I say that if a greater measure of judgment, of difficulties, of impediments and of toil do not make one art nobler than another, then painting and sculpture are the same thing and—in order that they may remain so—no painter should carve less than he paints and similarly no sculptor should paint less than he carves. By sculpture I mean to describe that which is done by carving out, for that which is done by adding is similar to painting. And since they both proceed from the same intelligence, they could be induced to make peace with one another and all these disputes abandoned, for they take up more time than is required to carve figures. As for the man who wrote that painting is a nobler art than sculpture, if he has thus understood all the other things he has written about, then better that my housemaid should have written them. There are infinite things that could be said, once and for all, about these arts, but, as I have explained, it would require too much time, and I have little, because I am not only old, but nearly dead, so please forgive me. I commend myself to you, and I thank you as much as I can and know how for the great honor you have done me, and of which I am unworthy. Yours,

MICHELANGELO BUONARROTI (1549?)

Leaving aside the fact that to this day he is the only man who has competently handled both the chisel and the brush; that there is no memory of the painting of ancient masters, while there endure many pieces of ancient sculpture, we may ask: who of those ancients was better than he? In the view of men of art, no one—unless we listen to the opinion of the vulgar masses who, without judging, admire antiquity because they envy the intelligence and industry of those ancients. Still I have yet to hear who would contradict me about this man, who has soared above envy. Raphael of Urbino, though he strove to compete with Michelangelo, has said many times that he thanked God for being born when he was, for he had learned from this man a different manner from the one of his father, who was a painter, and from that of Perugino, his master.

A. CONDIVI
Life of Michelangelo Buonarroti, 1553.

. . . four captives in the rough which serve to teach us how to carve figures from marble by a safe method that will not spoil the stone. This is the way: you take a figure in wax or some other solid material, and lay it horizontally in a vessel of water. Now water is, by its nature, flat and level at the surface and as you raise the said figure little by little from the level, so that it comes about that the prominent parts are revealed, while the other parts —those, namely, on the underside of the figure—remain hidden, until in the end it all comes into view. Figures must be chiselled out of marble in the same manner, first laying bare the more salient parts and then little by little the rest. This is the method followed by Michelangelo in the above-mentioned captives, which His Excellency wishes to be used as examples for his Academicians.

G. VASARI
The Lives, 1568.

About this matter (of roughing out) I can claim to have seen Michelangelo, aged more than sixty, and then not very strong, knocking more chips out of the hardest marble in a quarter of an hour than three young masons could have done in an hour, or even in an hour and a quarter. It seems incredible to anyone who has not actually seen it! He lunged at the marble with such fury that I feared lest the whole work would fall into pieces. With one blow he would remove chips as thick as three or four fingers, and his aim was so accurate that had he but chipped off a little more, all might have been ruined.

B. DE VIGNERE
in notes to *Images of the Two Philostrati*, 1579.

I have been induced to argue that the effect produced by Michelangelo's statues is partly due to some disproportions or unfinished parts which increase the importance of the finished ones. It seems to me—that if one may judge his paintings through their reproductions—that these do not show the same flaws in the same degree. I have often said to myself that Michelangelo, in spite of what he believed of himself, was more of a painter than a sculptor. He did not, in sculpture, proceed as the ancient masters did, that is, beginning with the masses, but he appeared to have traced everywhere an ideal outline, which he then filled in as painters do. It is as if his figure or his group came into his field of vision with one side only, which is what happens to painters. For this reason, the moment you change your viewing angle, which you must do in examining sculpture, you see distorted limbs, faulty planes —everything, in brief, that you do not see in the ancient masters.

E. DELACROIX
Diary, 1853.

Michelangelo was driven more powerfully than any other artist by the desire to re-create plastically, drawing out of his spirit, all the ephemera aspects, especially of the nude that are present in life and reconcilable with the higher dictates of style. In this he was at loggerheads with the ancient masters who allowed their themes to mature slowly and went on elaborating the same ones through five hundred years. Michelangelo, instead, was always trying to make use of new possibilities, and can therefore be described as the modern artist *par excellence*.

J. BURCKHARDT
The Cicerone, 1855.

[In the Bruges *Madonna and Child*] Michelangelo goes beyond all previous representations when he removes the Child from the Virgin's lap and places him, with an emphasis on size and weight, between her knees, where he almost gives the impression of climbing up his Mother's robe. By posing the Child as standing and moving, Michelangelo succeeded in increasing the plasticity of the group, and it then became quite natural for him to complicate the composition further by locating the Virgin's knees at two different levels. The Child is playing, but he is serious, much more serious than any Child previously sculpted, even if he was in the act of blessing. And so is the Madonna, thoughtful and silent; one would not dare speak to her. A deep, almost solemn seriousness envelops these two figures. . . .

The spirit of a new art is revealed in the Bruges *Madonna* with great strength and clarity. One may say that the vertical line of the head is in itself a motif, which for its greatness surpasses the whole spirit of the fifteenth century.

H. WÖLFFLIN
Classical Art, 1899.

Michelangelo summarizes, for all time, the artistic ideals of the Florentine Quattrocento. It is from the perfect fusion of the two stylistic tendencies, plastic-static and linear-dynamic, that his figures acquire their unmistakable quality of latent will and energy.

M. MARANGONI
Saper vedere, 1933.

Of all the arts Michelangelo preferred sculpture: it seemed to him that the art, within its well-defined boundaries, could express all the concepts of an artist; it was the art that responded best to his sensitivity, which obviously derived from the traditions of Florentine art, from Giotto to Masaccio, and had been raised by him into becoming a new powerful force; it was the art most suited to his absolutely visual ideals, entirely concentrated upon man and indifferent to any feature that was foreign to the human soul and form.

P. TOESCA
"Michelangelo" (in *Enciclopedia Italiana*), 1935.

Leonardo, with his *sfumato*, moves images away from our eyes and immerses them in atmosphere; Michelangelo knows no boundaries as he glorifies a figure's size and relief: with super-human energy he releases dynamic effects from intersections of planes and imparts to form the expression of his inner torment. A heroic seer, he sees no limits to his dreams of magnitude, of strength. The masses sculptured by him are colossal and hyper-bolic, but still fail to translate his fantasy of statues like towers and mountains.

A. VENTURI
La Scultura del Cinquecento, 1936.

His exaggerated plasticity . . . is beyond all schools, it is inimit-able and unattainable, because the style that constantly controls it is indissolubly linked to a life of great feeling.

A. BERTINI
Michelangelo fino alla Sistina, 1942.

The composition of the [Medici] Tombs represents the release of the spirit after death from the "earthly prison" of the body. The allegories of time—*Dawn*, *Dusk*, *Day* and *Night*—and those of the rivers of Hades (which were to be placed, in the original plan, beneath those of time) are the personifications of destiny. . . . These athletic figures reclining upon the sarcophagi of the Dukes seem, with their weight, to cause a break at the center of each marble cover, and through that break . . . the dead men's immor-tal souls escape to a region where they shall be secure from the blind forces of time. . . . There is an obvious resemblance between the concepts expressed in the Medici Chapel and Plato's concep-tion of death and immortality. In the *Phaedo* is described the life of a soul after death when, released from its prison, the spirit returns to a world for which it has longed. There, having reached its real home. the spirit is free to contemplate Ideas, just as we see, in the Chapel, the Dukes Michelangelo created, contemplat-ing the Virgin.

CHARLES DE TOLNAY
Michelangelo, 1951.

75

BIBLIOGRAPHICAL NOTE

The extensive literature on Michelangelo is listed up to 1926 in the *Michelangelo Bibliographie* by E. Steinmann and R. Wittkower (Leipzig, 1927), updated to 1930 by Steinmann himself in the appendix to his book, *Michelangelo im Spiegel seiner Zeit* (Leipzig, 1930, pp. 65–95). Later P. Cherubelli compiled a bibliography covering the period from 1931 to 1942 for the volume of essays *Michelangelo Buonarroti nel IV Centenario dello scoprimento del Giudizio Universale* (Michelangelo Buonarroti on the Fourth Centenary of the Unveiling of the Last Judgment) (Florence, 1942, pp. 270 ff.). The most important works published in the following decade are listed in the bibliography of Charles de Tolnay's five-volume *Michelangelo* (Princeton University Press, 1943–60).

The reader can obtain relevant information about the principal editions of Michelangelo's own writings, as well as about publications on his life and works that have been published from the sixteenth century to the present in *All the Paintings of Michelangelo* by Enzo Carli in this same series.

Among the most important works on Michelangelo's sculpture, the following should be consulted:

E. GUILLAUME. "Michel-Ange sculpteur," in *Gazette des Beaux-Arts*, 1876.
C. MALLARMÉ. *L'ultima tragedia di Michelangelo*, Rome, 1929.
F. BAUMGART. "Die Pietà Rondanini," in *Jahrbuch der preussischen Kunstammlungen*, 1935.
A. VENTURI. *La Scultura del Cinquecento*, Milan, 1936.
E. PANOFSKY. "The First Projects of Michelangelo's Tomb of Julius II," in *Art Bulletin*, 1937.
P. TOESCA. "Un capolavoro di Michelangelo: la Pietà di Palestrina," in *Le Arti*, 1938–39.
F. KRIEGBAUM. "Michelangelo Buonarroti," in *Die Bildwerke*, Berlin, 1940.
F. KRIEGBAUM. "Le statue di Michelangelo nell'Aftare dei Piccolomini a Siena," in *Michelangelo Buonarroti nel IV Centenario dello scoprimento de Giudizio Universale*, Florence, 1942.
C. L. RAGGHIANTI. "Michelangelo gratuito," in *Miscellanea minore di critica d'arte*, Bari, 1946.
C. DE TOLNAY. *Michelangelo*, Volume III: *The Medici Chapel*, Princeton, 1948.
J. ALAZARD. *Les Sculpteurs de Michel-Ange*, Paris, 1949.
L. GOLDSCHEIDER. *The Sculptures of Michelangelo*, London, 1950.

Concerning the question of the unfinished works, the following articles should be consulted:

A. BERTINI. "Il problema del non finito nell'arte di Michelangelo," in *L'Arte*, 1930.
V. MARIANI. "L''aspra catena' in Michelangelo," in *La Cultura*, 1931.

A. BERTINI. "Ancora sul non finito di Michelangelo," in *L'Arte*, 1931.

V. MARIANI. "Note michelangiolesche," in *L'Arte*, 1931.

A. BERTINI. "A proposito di note michelangiolesche," in *L'Arte*, 1931.

S. BETTINI. "Sul non finito in Michelangelo," in *La Nuova Italia*, VI, 1935.

C. ARU. "La veduta unica e il problema del non finito in Michelangelo," in *L'Arte*, 1937.

V. MARIANI. "La Pietà di Palestrina a Roma," in *L'Arte*, 1939.

REPRODUCTIONS

ACKNOWLEDGEMENT FOR PLATES

Plates 1, 7, 36–37, 40–43, and 110: *Alinari, Florence*. Plates 2, 29, 66–68, 72, 74–75, 83–84, 88, 114, 116, 118, and 121: *Director of the Florence Gallery*. Plates 3–6, 12–14, 22–25, 27, 31–32, 34–35, 44, 46–53, 56–65, 69, 73, 76–77, 79–82, 85–87, 89–91, 94–109, 115, 117, 119–20, and 126: *Brogi, Florence*. Plates 8–9: *Croci, Bologna*. Plate 10: *Villani, Bologna*. Plates 11, 17, 26, 30, 45, 54–55, 70–71, 78, 111–12, and 127: *Anderson, Rome*. Plates 18–21: *A.C.L., Brussels*. Plate 33: *Royal Academy, London*. Plates 38–39: *Scarnati, Paris*. Plate 122: *Pagano Archives, Milan*. Plates 124–25: *Bacci, Milan*.

The photographs of plates 2, 8, 12, 15, 27, 82–84 are reproduced here through the kind permission of Professor Charles de Tolnay.

Plate I. MADONNA OF THE STAIRS, Florence, Casa Buonarroti

Plate 2. THE BATTLE OF CENTAURS, Florence, Casa Buonarroti

Plate 3. *Detail of plate 2*

Plate 4. *Detail of plate 2*

Plate 5. *Detail of plate 2*

Plate 6. ST PROCULUS, Bologna, Basilica of San Domenico

Plate 7. ST PETRONIUS, Bologna, Basilica of San Domenico

Plate 8. ANGEL HOLDING A CANDLESTICK, Bologna,
Basilica of San Domenico

Plate 9. ANGEL HOLDING A CANDLESTICK, front view

Plate 10. *Detail of plate 9*

Plate 11. BACCHUS, Florence, Museo Nazionale (Bargello)

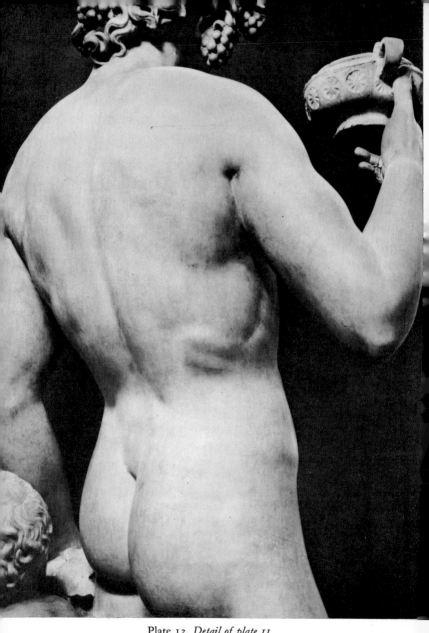

Plate 12. *Detail of plate 11*

Plate 13. *Detail of plate 11*

Plate 14. PIETÀ, Rome, Basilica of St Peter

Plate 15. *Detail of plate 14*

Plate 16. *Detail of plate 14*

Plate 17. *Detail of plate 14*

Plate 18. MADONNA AND CHILD, Bruges, Church of Notre-Dame

Plate 19. MADONNA AND CHILD, front view

Plate 20. *Detail of plate 18*

Plate 21. *Detail of plate 18*

Plate 22. ST PAUL, Siena, Duomo, Piccolomini Altar

Plate 23. ST PETER, Siena, Duomo, Piccolomini Altar

Plate 24. ST PIUS, Siena, Duomo, Piccolomini Altar

Plate 25. ST GREGORY, Siena, Duomo, Piccolomini Altar

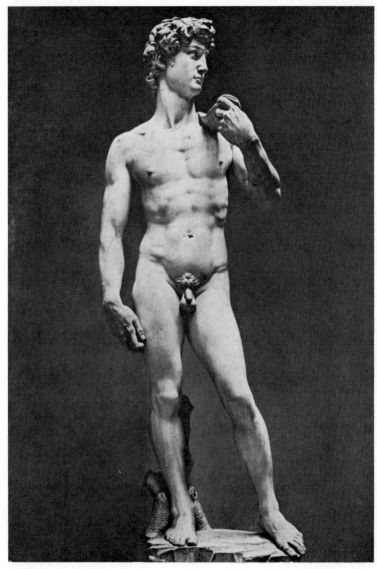

Plate 26. DAVID, Florence, Galleria dell'Accademia di Belle Arti

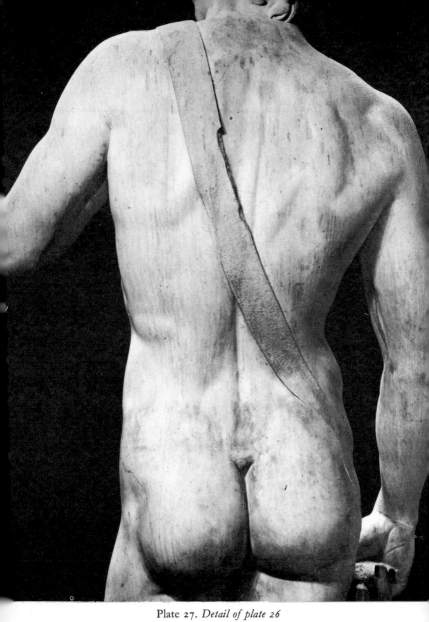

Plate 27. *Detail of plate 26*

Plate 28. *Detail of plate 26*

Plate 29. *Detail of plate 26*

Plate 30. THE PITTI MADONNA, Florence, Museo Nazionale (Bargello)

Plate 31. *Detail of plate 30*

Plate 32. *Detail of plate 30*

LORENZO DE' MEDICI,
Florence, Basilica of San Lorenzo
(*detail of plate 50*)

Plate 33. THE TADDEI MADONNA, London, Royal Academy

Plate 34. ST MATTHEW, Florence, Galleria dell'Accademia
di Belle Arti

Plate 35. *Detail of plate 34*

Plate 36. THE DYING SLAVE, Paris, Louvre

Plate 37. THE REBELLIOUS SLAVE, Paris, Louvre

Plate 38. *Detail of plate 36*

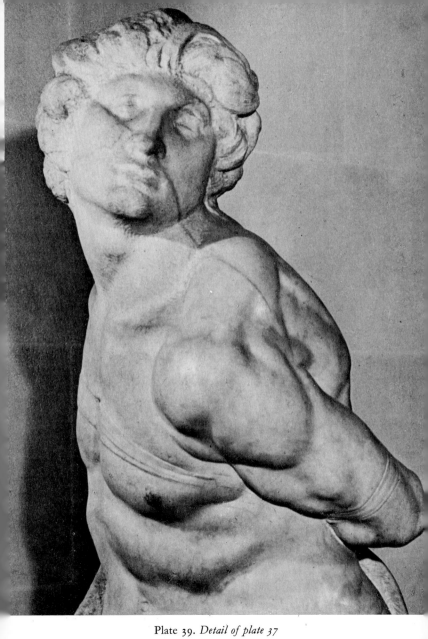

Plate 39. *Detail of plate 37*

Plate 40. MOSES, Rome, Church of San Pietro in Vincoli

Plate 41. MOSES, from the right

Plate 42. *Detail of plate 40*

Plate 43. *Detail of plate 40*

Plate 44. HERCULES AND CACUS, Florence, Casa Buonarroti

Plate 45. THE RISEN CHRIST,
Rome, Church of Santa Maria sopra Minerva

Plate 46. TOMB OF LORENZO DE' MEDICI, DUKE OF URBINO,
Florence, Basilica of San Lorenzo

Plate 47. TOMB OF GIULIANO DE' MEDICI, DUKE OF NEMOURS,
Florence, Basilica of San Lorenzo

Plate 48. TOMB OF LORENZO DE' MEDICI, DUKE OF URBINO,
side view

Plate 49. TOMB OF GIULIANO DE' MEDICI, DUKE OF NEMOURS, side view

Plate 50. LORENZO DE' MEDICI, Florence, Basilica of San Lorenzo

Plate 51. *Detail of plate 50*

Plate 52. *Detail of plate 50*

Plate 53. *Detail of plate 50*

Plate 54. DUSK, Florence, Basilica of San Lorenzo

Plate 55. DAWN, Florence, Basilica of San Lorenzo

Plate 56. DUSK, rear view

Plate 57. DAWN, rear view

Plate 58. DUSK, side view

Plate 59. DAWN, side view

Plate 60. *Detail of plate 54*

Plate 61. *Detail of plate 55*

Plate 62. *Detail of plate 55*

Plate 63. *Detail of plate 55*

Plate 64. *Detail of plate 54*

Plate 65. GIULIANO DE' MEDICI, Florence, Basilica of San Lorenzo

Plate 66. GIULIANO DE' MEDICI, rear view

Plate 67. *Detail of plate 65*

Plate 68. *Detail of plate 66*

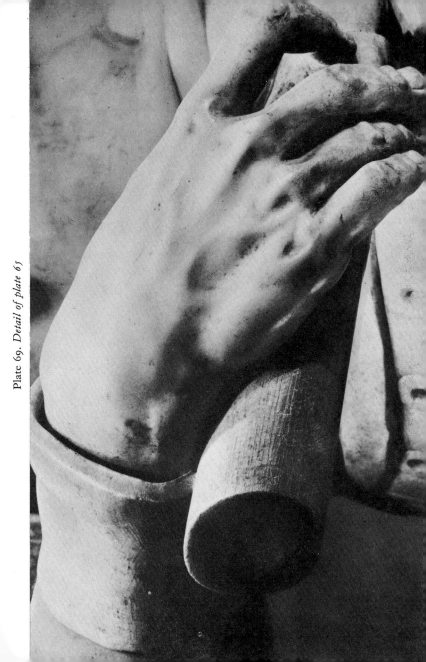

Plate 69. *Detail of plate 65*

Plate 70. NIGHT, Florence, Basilica of San Lorenzo

Plate 71. DAY, Florence, Basilica of San Lorenzo

Plate 72. NIGHT, rear view

Plate 73. DAY, rear view

Plate 74. NIGHT, side view

Plate 75. DAY, side view

Plate 76. *Detail of plate 70*

Plate 77. *Detail of plate 70*

Plate 78. *Detail of plate 70*

Plate 79. *Detail of plate 70*

Plate 80. *Detail of plate 71*

Plate 81. *Detail of plate 71*

Plate 82. FRIEZES IN THE MEDICI CHAPEL,
Florence, Basilica of San Lorenzo

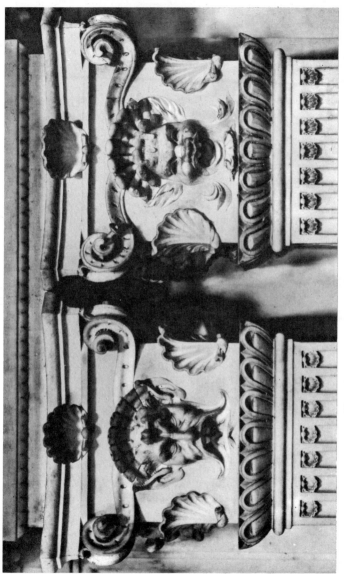

Plate 83. FRIEZES IN THE MEDICI CHAPEL,
Florence, Basilica of San Lorenzo

Plate 84. FRIEZES IN THE MEDICI CHAPEL,
Florence, Basilica of San Lorenzo

Plate 85. ENTRANCE WALL OF THE MEDICI CHAPEL,
Florence, Basilica of San Lorenzo

Plate 86. MADONNA AND CHILD, Florence, Basilica of San Lorenzo, Medici Chapel

Plate 87. MADONNA AND CHILD, front view

Plate 88. *Detail of plate 86*

Plate 89. *Detail of plate 86*

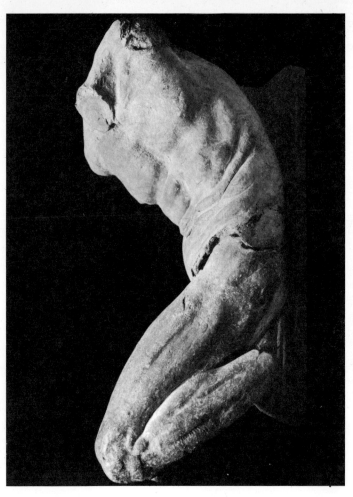

Plate 90. MODEL FOR A RIVER GOD, Florence,
Galleria dell'Accademia di Belle Arti

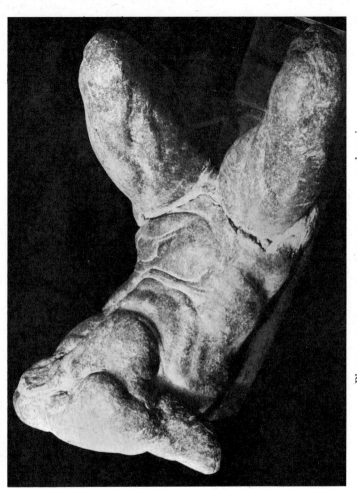

Plate 91. MODEL FOR A RIVER GOD, another view

Plate 92. THE CROUCHING BOY, Leningrad, Hermitage

Plate 93. THE CROUCHING BOY, side view

Plate 94. DAVID-APOLLO, Florence, Museo Nazionale (Bargello)

Plate 95. DAVID-APOLLO, side view

Plate 96. THE VICTORY, Florence, Signoria Palace

BRUTUS,
Florence, Museo Nazionale, Bargello
(*detail of plate 108*)

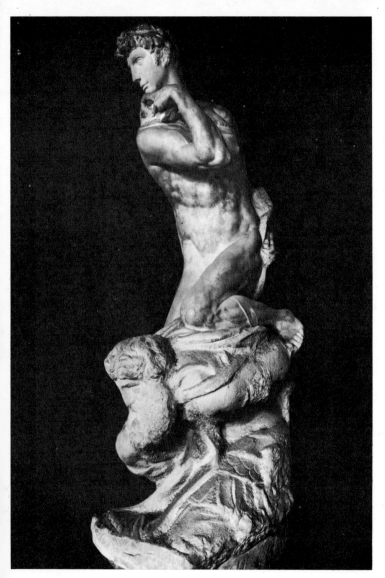

Plate 97. THE VICTORY, side view

Plate 98. *Detail of plate 96*

Plate 99. *Detail of plate 96*

Plate 100. YOUTHFUL CAPTIVE, Florence, Galleria dell'Accademia
di Belle Arti

Plate 101. YOUTHFUL CAPTIVE, side view

Plate 102. BEARDED CAPTIVE, Florence, Galleria dell'Accademia di Belle Arti

Plate 103. BEARDED CAPTIVE, side view

Plate 104. ATLAS, Florence, Galleria dell'Accademia di Belle Arti

Plate 105. ATLAS, side view

Plate 106. AWAKENING CAPTIVE, Florence, Galleria dell'Accademia
di Belle Arti

Plate 107. AWAKENING CAPTIVE, side view

Plate 108. BRUTUS, Florence, Museo Nazionale (Bargello)

Plate 109. *Detail of plate 108*

Plate 110. TOMB OF JULIUS II, Rome, Basilica of San Pietro in Vincoli

Plate III. RACHEL, Rome, Basilica of San Pietro in Vincoli, Tomb
of Julius II

Plate 112. LEAH, Rome, Basilica of San Pietro in Vincoli, Tomb
of Julius II

RONDANINI PIETA,
Milan, Civiche Raccolte d'Arte, Castello Sforzesco
(*detail of plate 123*)

Plate 113. *Detail of plate 112*

Plate 114. PIETÀ, Florence, Duomo

Plate 115. PIETÀ, front view

Plate 116. PIETÀ, rear view

Plate 117. *Detail of plate 114*

Plate 118. *Detail of plate 114*

Plate 119. PALESTRINA PIETÀ, Florence, Galleria dell'Accademia di Belle Arti

Plate 120. *Detail of plate 119*

Plate 121. *Detail of plate 119*

Plate 122. *Detail of plate 119*

Plate 123. RONDANINI PIETÀ, Milan, Civiche Raccolte d'Arte
(Castello Sforzesco)

Plate 124. RONDANINI PIETÀ, another view

Plate 125. RONDANINI PIETÀ, side view

Plate 126. RONDANINI PIETÀ, side view

Plate 127. *Detail of plate 123*

Plate 128. *Detail of plate 123*